POEMS ON
THE UNDERGROUND

POEMS
ON THE
UNDERGROUND

ILLUSTRATED EDITION

edited by
Gerard Benson
Judith Chernaik
Cicely Herbert

CASSELL

Cassell Publishers Limited
Villiers House, 41/47 Strand
London WC2N 5JE

Introduction, selection and editorial matter
copyright © Poems on the Underground 1991, 1992
Poems copyright authors and publishers (see Acknowledgements)
Posters copyright © London Transport Museum 1992

First published in this edition 1992

British Library Cataloguing in Publication Data
A catalogue record for this book is available from the British Library

ISBN 0–304–34252–1

Distributed in Australia by
Capricorn Link (Australia) Pty Ltd
PO Box 665, Lane Cove, NSW 2066

Distributed in the United States by
Sterling Publishing Co, Inc.
387 Park Avenue South, New York, NY 10016–8810

Typeset in Monophoto Meridien by
August Filmsetting, Haydock, St Helens

Printed and bound in Great Britain by
Mackays of Chatham PLC, Chatham, Kent

CONTENTS

List of Illustrations   *page* 13
List of Underground Posters   15
Introduction   17
Introduction to the Illustrated Edition   21

THE POEMS

Up in the Morning Early   25
Robert Burns (1759–96)
Ozymandias   26
Percy Bysshe Shelley (1792–1822)
This Is Just to Say   27
William Carlos Williams (1883–1963)
The Railway Children   28
Seamus Heaney (b. 1939)
Like a Beacon   29
Grace Nichols (b. 1950)

Sonnet 29   30
William Shakespeare (1564–1616)
Her Anxiety   31
W. B. Yeats (1865–1939)
Lady 'Rogue' Singleton   32
Stevie Smith (1902–71)
The Trees   33
Philip Larkin (1922–85)
Benediction   34
James Berry (b. 1924)

The Sick Rose   35
William Blake (1757–1827)
'Much Madness is divinest Sense'   36
Emily Dickinson (1830–86)

At Lord's 37
Francis Thompson (1859–1907)
Rainforest 38
Judith Wright (b. 1915)
Encounter at St. Martin's 39
Ken Smith (b. 1938)

'Western wind when wilt thou blow' 40
Anon. (early 16th century)
**Composed Upon Westminster Bridge,
September 3, 1802** 41
William Wordsworth (1770–1850)
Everyone Sang 42
Siegfried Sassoon (1886–1967)
The Loch Ness Monster's Song 43
Edwin Morgan (b. 1920)
Living 44
Denise Levertov (b. 1923)

Holy Sonnet 45
('Death be not proud, though some have called thee')
John Donne (1572–1631)
'Trail all your pikes' 46
Anne Finch, Countess of Winchilsea (1661–1720)
Alas, Alack! 47
Walter de la Mare (1873–1956)
Immigrant 48
Fleur Adcock (b. 1934)
I Am Becoming My Mother 49
Lorna Goodison (b. 1947)

'Tagus farewell' 50
Sir Thomas Wyatt (1503–42)
Snow 51
Edward Thomas (1878–1917)
Lines *from* **Endymion** 53
John Keats (1795–1821)

Celia Celia 54
Adrian Mitchell (b. 1932)
Goodbye 54
Adrian Mitchell
Ragwort 55
Anne Stevenson (b. 1933)

'The silver swan' 56
Anon. (*c.*1600)
'So we'll go no more a-roving' 57
George Gordon, Lord Byron (1788–1824)
Teeth 58
Spike Milligan (b. 1918)
To My First White Hairs 59
Wole Soyinka (b. 1935)
Riddle-Me-Ree 60
Liz Lochhead (b. 1947)

The Expulsion from Eden *from* **Paradise Lost,
Book XII** 61
John Milton (1608–74)
'There was an Old Man with a beard' 62
Edward Lear (1812–88)
Spring and Fall 63
Gerard Manley Hopkins (1844–89)
Dog Days 64
Derek Mahon (b. 1941)
The Visitor 65
Carolyn Forché (b. 1950)

Ariel's Song 66
William Shakespeare (1564–1616)
Meeting at Night 67
Robert Browning (1812–89)
Prelude I 68
T. S. Eliot (1888–1965)

London Airport 69
Christopher Logue (b. 1926)
Taid's Grave 70
Gillian Clarke (b. 1937)

The Coming of Grendel *from* **Beowulf** 71
translated by Gerard Benson
In my Craft or Sullen Art 72
Dylan Thomas (1914–53)
Midsummer, Tobago 73
Derek Walcott (b. 1930)
Sonnet from the Portuguese 75
('How do I love thee? Let me count the ways')
Elizabeth Barrett Browning (1806–61)
Handbag 76
Ruth Fainlight (b. 1931)

Symphony in Yellow 77
Oscar Wilde (1854–1900)
'Sumer is icumen in' 79
Anon. (13th century)
Song 80
('Stop all the clocks, cut off the telephone')
W. H. Auden (1907–73)
The Ancients of the World 81
R. S. Thomas (b. 1913)
Day Trip 82
Carole Satyamurti (b. 1939)

In Time of 'The Breaking of Nations' 83
Thomas Hardy (1840–1928)
London Bells 84
Anon. (early 18th century)
The Tyger 87
William Blake (1757–1827)
Delay 88
Elizabeth Jennings (b. 1926)

Everything Changes   89
Cicely Herbert (b. 1937)

Roundel *from* **The Parliament of Fowls**   90
Geoffrey Chaucer (1340?–1400)
Dreams   91
Robert Herrick (1591–1674)
Sonnet   92
('What lips my lips have kissed, and where, and why')
Edna St. Vincent Millay (1892–1950)
And Yet the Books   93
Czeslaw Milosz (b. 1911), *translated by* Czeslaw Milosz and
Robert Hass
The Leader   94
Roger McGough (b. 1937)

from **To the City of London**   95
William Dunbar (1465?–1530?)
On First Looking into Chapman's Homer   96
John Keats (1795–1821)
A Dead Statesman   97
Rudyard Kipling (1865–1936)
Modern Secrets   98
Shirley Geok-lin Lim (b. 1944)
Sergeant Brown's Parrot   99
Kit Wright (b. 1944)

'I have a gentil cock'   100
Anon. (early 15th century)
What Am I After All   101
Walt Whitman (1819–92)
Piano   102
D. H. Lawrence (1885–1930)
Mmenson   103
Edward Kamau Brathwaite (b. 1930)
Light   104
Diane Wakoski (b. 1937)

from **The Song of Solomon** 105
The King James Bible (1611)
'You took away all the oceans and all the room' 106
Osip Mandelstam (1891–1938), *translated by* Clarence
Brown and W. S. Merwin
Wet Evening in April 107
Patrick Kavanagh (1906–67)
I Saw a Jolly Hunter 108
Charles Causley (b. 1917)
Aunt Jennifer's Tigers 109
Adrienne Rich (b. 1929)

Old English Riddle 110
translated by Gerard Benson
Virtue 111
George Herbert (1593–1633)
'I know the truth – give up all other truths!' 112
Marina Tsvetayeva (1892–1941), *translated by*
Elaine Feinstein
Love Without Hope 113
Robert Graves (1895–1985)
Full Moon and Little Frieda 114
Ted Hughes (b. 1930)

'Since there's no hope, come let us kiss and part' 115
Michael Drayton (1563–1631)
'Into my heart an air that kills' 116
A. E. Housman (1859–1936)
Dolor 117
Theodore Roethke (1908–63)
The Cries of London 118
Anon. (17th century)
A 14-Year-Old Convalescent Cat in the Winter 120
Gavin Ewart (b. 1916)
Come. And Be My Baby 121
Maya Angelou (b. 1928)

'Ich am of Irlonde' 122
Anon. (14th century)
Song 123
('Now sleeps the crimson petal, now the white')
Alfred, Lord Tennyson (1809–92)
The Embankment 124
(The Fantasia of a Fallen Gentleman on a Cold, Bitter Night)
T. E. Hulme (1883–1917)
Stars and planets 125
Norman MacCaig (b. 1910)
The Uncertainty of the Poet 126
Wendy Cope (b. 1945)

'I saw a Peacock with a fiery tail' 127
Anon. (17th century)
from **Frost at Midnight** 128
Samuel Taylor Coleridge (1772–1834)
Snow 129
Louis MacNeice (1907–63)
On Himself 130
David Wright (b. 1920)
Sometimes 131
Sheenagh Pugh (b. 1950)

The Passionate Shepherd to his Love 132
Christopher Marlowe (1564–93)
Letter to André Billy. 9 April 1915 133
Guillaume Apollinaire (1880–1918), *translated by*
Oliver Bernard
Child 134
Sylvia Plath (1932–63)
A song for England 135
Andrew Salkey (b. 1928)
Letters from Yorkshire 136
Maura Dooley (b. 1957)

The Bonnie Broukit Bairn   137
Hugh MacDiarmid (Christopher Murray Grieve)
(1892–1978)
To Emilia V–   139
Percy Bysshe Shelley (1792–1822)
Concerto for Double Bass   140
John Fuller (b. 1937)
Words, Wide Night   141
Carol Ann Duffy (b. 1955)
The Lobster Quadrille   142
Lewis Carroll (1832–98)

'I shall say what inordinate love is'   144
Anon. (15th century)
A red red rose   145
Robert Burns (1759–96)
The Very Leaves of the Acacia-Tree are London   146
Kathleen Raine (b. 1908)
One Art   147
Elizabeth Bishop (1911–79)
To Someone Who Insisted I Look Up Someone   148
X. J. Kennedy (b. 1929)

Notes to the Poems   149
Notes to the Posters   161
Index of Poets, Authors and Translators   171
Index of First Lines   173
A Note of Thanks   177
Acknowledgements   179

LIST OF ILLUSTRATIONS

1   Westron wynde when wilt thou blow   *page* 40
2   Alas, Alack!   47
3   'Tagus farewell'   50
4   Endymion   52
5   The silver Swanne   56
6   Teeth   58
7   There was an Old Man with a beard   62
8   'How do I love thee?'   74
9   Caricature of Oscar Wilde in a Top Hat   77
10 'Sumer is icumen in'   78
11 London Bells   85
12 The Tyger   86
13 Introduction to *The Parliament of Fowls*   90
14 To the City of London   95
15 Sergeant Brown's Parrot   99
16 I Saw a Jolly Hunter   108
17 Old English Riddle from *The Exeter Book*.   110
18 The Cries of London. Setting by Orlando Gibbons   119
19 'Music, when soft voices die'   138
20 The Lobster Quadrille   143
21 'I shall say what inordinate love is'   144

LIST OF UNDERGROUND POSTERS

following page 28
1   Pied Piper
2   The Only Way to the Theatres
3   'As we dance round a-ring-a-ring'
4   'Over the land freckled with snow half-thawed'

following page 60
Humours of London
5   At the Shops
6   'Appy 'Ampstead
7   At the Proms
8   Up River

following page 76
Flowers and Forests
9   Flowers of the Riverside
10   Flowers o' the Corn
11   Blue Bells, Kew Gardens
12   The Forest Glades of Epping

following page 92
Home Counties
13   Essex
14   Bucks
15   Surrey
16   Kent

following page 124
The Proud City
17   St. Paul's
18   St. Clement Danes

19 Temple Church and Library
20 Chelsea Power House

following page 140
21 The River Colne, Uxbridge
22 The Daffodils are Out
23 'Spring goeth all in white'
24 Book to Golder's Green

INTRODUCTION

ANYONE who suffers from an addiction to reading cereal box tops or bus tickets will understand the special appeal of 'Poems on the Underground'. The programme began as an idea shared among a few friends: how pleasant it would be', we thought, to read a few lines by one's favourite poet on the Tube, instead of advertisements for mints or temps. We were Londoners by birth or adoption, habitual users of public transport, lovers of poetry. We shared the conviction that poetry is a popular, living art, and that the pleasures of rhythm and rhyme are part of common life. The Underground, also an inescapable part of our common life, had large numbers of empty advertising spaces. It seemed an entirely reasonable idea to propose filling the blank grey slots with poems, for the entertainment of the travelling public.

London Underground was surprisingly responsive to our suggestion that they provide unlet spaces free for this civic purpose. They agreed that if we could raise money to pay a modest charge for five hundred spaces, they would match the number. With an Arts Council grant from the Compton Poetry Fund, set up 'for the wider dissemination of poetry', and generous support from the publishers Faber and Faber, who produced the posters for the first two years, and Oxford University Press, who provided matching funds, we presented the first group of poems to an unsuspecting public.

On Wednesday, 29 January 1986, 'Poems on the Underground' was officially launched at Aldwych, a station usually closed between rush hours, and often used for filming movies about the Second World War. Many of those who descended to the Underground platform that rain-drenched morning might have had in mind the journey made to the infernal regions by Orpheus in search of Eurydice. Ordinary signs – TICKETS AND TRAINS, THIS WAY DOWN, STAND CLEAR, DOORS CLOSING – assume a special significance when such a setting is taken over by poets and their friends. Official party fare was coffee and doughnuts, but wine flowed too, and when the train bearing its consignment of poems arrived, twenty minutes late, we all climbed aboard, pursued by representatives of the press, radio and television. Within minutes the carriages were alive to the sounds of happy poets declaiming verse by Shelley, Burns and, of course, by themselves.

When we began to scatter poems about in public, we had no idea how people would respond; it was all a bit reminiscent of the lovesick youth in the Forest of Arden, hanging 'odes upon hawthorns and elegies on brambles'. Not that the London Underground is anything like the Forest of Arden; on the contrary, it is the ultimate expression of the modern urban working world. But poetry thrives on paradox, and the poems seemed to take on new and surprising life when they were removed from books and set amongst the adverts. Commuters enjoyed the idea of reading Keats's 'Much have I travell'd in the realms of gold' on a crowded Central Line train, or trying to memorise a sonnet between Leicester Square and Hammersmith. Just as we had hoped, the poems provided relief, caused smiles, offered refreshment to the soul – and all in a place where one would least expect to find anything remotely poetic.

The truth, as we soon discovered, is that England is a nation of poetry-lovers. Hundreds of people wrote in with queries about particular poems, suggestions of their own, and comments; many letters just said, in effect, 'Thank you, whoever you are, for the poems.' Three years after our launch, London Underground agreed to provide all spaces free and to quadruple the number, in theory providing at least one poem to each train carriage, and to pay production costs as well. Posters go to British Council libraries throughout the world, and the London Transport Museum maintains a subscription list, mainly for schools and libraries, but also for hospitals, community centres and prisons. We are set to continue indefinitely, and there seems no possibility of running out of poems, either from the past or by contemporary poets.

From the start, we have tried to offer as wide a variety of tone and subject matter as possible, to share our own favourites and our special discoveries, but also to present new voices. At least two poems out of each group of five (occasionally six) are by living poets. We have taken material from the earliest times to the present, and we have made a point of including poets from English-speaking countries throughout the world. A few translations are also included, and 'Anon.' features largely, in songs and riddles, nursery rhymes and broadside ballads.

We have kept a special place for London poems, and for poets who had close associations with London – Donne, Milton, Blake and Keats, among others – though some of the most celebrated London poems (like 'To the City of London', by the Scottish poet William Dunbar, and Wordsworth's 'Composed Upon Westminster Bridge') were written by poets as they were passing through. Of London poems in our collection by contemporary writers, one is by the New Zealand-born poet Fleur Adcock, another by the Guyanese poet Grace Nichols. Then again, A. E. Housman wrote *A Shropshire Lad* when he was working every day at the Chancery Lane Patent Office; and we have assumed that the imagination is free to wander where it will. What we have listened for is the individual voice, and we have tried to offer poems in which the poet's voice speaks directly to the modern reader about the common themes of poetry through the ages.

The great subjects are well represented here: love, death, war, the natural world, time, memory. But these are not the only themes of poetry, nor is the high-flown the only mode. There is also a fine tradition of comic verse, and in amongst the passion and nostalgia we placed a few banana skins in the form of light, humorous and quirky verse. We have included writers of comic nonsense like Edward Lear, Spike Milligan and Wendy Cope; there are also pieces in a witty, conversational vein by poets ranging from Michael Drayton and William Carlos Williams to Stevie Smith and Liz Lochhead. Some light or funny verse was chosen with children in mind, but we found that these poems often appealed as much to adults as to children; Roger McGough's 'The Leader' found its way into a number of boardrooms and political party headquarters.

The programme has now been in existence for five years and has spawned a number of associated projects. In November of our first year, we organised a gathering of poets for a twelve-hour Remembrance Day reading in St James's Church, Piccadilly, at which more than ninety people contributed readings and music from all over the world. A further venture was made possible by a grant from the Calouste Gulbenkian Foundation, which twice enabled us to fill every advertising space in a train carriage with poems written by schoolchildren. These were chosen initially from work produced in London school workshops; a second selection was made from the huge entry received in workshops and competitions organised by the Poetry Society, the BBC Radio 5 programme *Talking Poetry* and the 'Young Telegraph'. We have also given annual readings at the British Library, as part of the Stefan Zweig Series, with programmes that draw on the Library's collections. Poems featured on the Tube have often been broadcast and discussed on local radio and also on the BBC World Service, reaching audiences as far afield as Bulgaria and Japan. Similar projects have sprung up elsewhere in Britain and abroad, with poems riding public transport systems in Newcastle, West Yorkshire, Dublin and Stuttgart, and decorating bus and railway platforms in Vienna and Melbourne.

This anthology has come about in response to public interest in the programme, and in particular poems that appeared briefly on the Tube and then vanished from sight, leaving only a memory of a single line or image. They are all here (with one substitution) in the order in which they appeared on the Tube, in groups of five or six. Many of the poems will be familiar to readers; others are fairly obscure and hard to find without special library resources; some are unique to this volume. We hope that the collection as a whole will appeal not only to addicted poetry-lovers but also to readers who are coming to poetry for the first time.

Gerard Benson, Judith Chernaik, Cicely Herbert
London, 1991

INTRODUCTION TO
THE ILLUSTRATED EDITION

IN THIS new and expanded illustrated edition of *Poems on the Underground*, we include fifteen poems which have been displayed on Underground trains during the past year, along with twenty-four historic Underground posters featuring poetry or, occasionally, prose. These early posters celebrate the city in all its 'Humours'; they invite the travelling public to enjoy the urban pleasures of theatres, concerts, shops, parks and playgrounds or, better still, to explore the surrounding countryside. The earliest posters in our selection are from 1911, when London's chaotic system of omnibuses, electric tramways and Underground railways was moving towards a single consolidated management; the most recent posters are taken from an evocative series of 1944, 'The Proud City', celebrating London's survival through the massive bombing raids of the Second World War.

The extracts used to illustrate the posters reflect the wide-ranging taste of an earlier time, shaped by anthologies like Palgrave's *Golden Treasury* and the popular reprints of Everyman's Library. Someone within the Underground loved poetry and knew the classics well. Romantic and Victorian poets (Wordsworth, Shelley and Byron, Tennyson and Browning) were favourites, along with Shakespeare and Milton. Of contemporary poets, the most popular was Robert Bridges, poet laureate from 1913 to 1930. Whoever made the selections had a sense of humour; it takes a special kind of wit to present the Pied Piper enticing children into the depths of the Underground, and to advertise the charms of Oxford Street with Wordsworth's sonnet, 'The world is too much with us' ('Getting and spending we lay waste our powers' – At the Shops).

All of which suggests that poetry can always take on new life in a new context. We identify sources and indicate the original context in our notes to the posters on page 161.

We continue to receive support, encouragement, and suggestions for poems from a large and generous readership, to whom we say: long may poetry flourish, on the Underground, on the printed page, and in the hearts and minds of the people.

G.B., J.C., C.H.
London, 1992

THE POEMS

Up in the Morning Early

Cauld blaws the wind frae east to west,
  The drift is driving sairly;
Sae loud and shrill's I hear the blast,
  I'm sure it's winter fairly.

CHORUS: Up in the morning's no for me,
  Up in the morning early;
When a' the hills are cover'd wi' snaw,
  I'm sure it's winter fairly.

The birds sit chittering in the thorn,
  A' day they fare but sparely;
And lang's the night frae e'en to morn,
  I'm sure it's winter fairly.

CHORUS: Up in the morning's no for me,
  Up in the morning early;
When a' the hills are cover'd wi' snaw,
  I'm sure it's winter fairly.

ROBERT BURNS (1759–96)

Ozymandias

I met a traveller from an antique land
Who said: Two vast and trunkless legs of stone
Stand in the desert . . . Near them, on the sand,
Half sunk, a shattered visage lies, whose frown,
And wrinkled lip, and sneer of cold command,
Tell that its sculptor well those passions read
Which yet survive, stamped on these lifeless things,
The hand that mocked them and the heart that fed;
And on the pedestal these words appear:
"My name is OZYMANDIAS, king of kings:
Look on my works, ye Mighty, and despair!"
Nothing beside remains. Round the decay
Of that colossal wreck, boundless and bare
The lone and level sands stretch far away.

PERCY BYSSHE SHELLEY (1792–1822)

This Is Just to Say

I have eaten
the plums
that were in
the icebox

and which
you were probably
saving
for breakfast

Forgive me
they were delicious
so sweet
and so cold

WILLIAM CARLOS WILLIAMS (1883–1963)

The Railway Children

When we climbed the slopes of the cutting
We were eye-level with the white cups
Of the telegraph poles and the sizzling wires.

Like lovely freehand they curved for miles
East and miles west beyond us, sagging
Under their burden of swallows.

We were small and thought we knew nothing
Worth knowing. We thought words travelled the wires
In the shiny pouches of raindrops,

Each one seeded full with the light
Of the sky, the gleam of the lines, and ourselves
So infinitesimally scaled

We could stream through the eye of a needle.

SEAMUS HEANEY (b. 1939)

1 *Pied Piper* **Dora McLaren** 1914

2 *The Only Way to the Theatres* **Artist unknown** 1911

3 *'As we dance round a-ring-a-ring'* **A. E. Marty** 1931

Over the land freckled with snow half-thawed
The speculating rooks at their nests cawed
And saw from elm-tops, delicate as flower of grass,
What we below could not see, Winter pass.

EDWARD THOMAS

4 *'Over the land freckled with snow half-thawed'* **C. R. W. Nevinson** 1939

Like a Beacon

In London
every now and then
I get this craving
for my mother's food
I leave art galleries
in search of plantains
saltfish/sweet potatoes

I need this link

I need this touch
of home
swinging my bag
like a beacon
against the cold

GRACE NICHOLS (b. 1950)

Sonnet 29

When in disgrace with Fortune and men's eyes,
I all alone beweep my outcast state,
And trouble deaf heaven with my bootless cries,
And look upon myself and curse my fate,
Wishing me like to one more rich in hope,
Featured like him, like him with friends possessed,
Desiring this man's art, and that man's scope,
With what I most enjoy contented least,
Yet in these thoughts myself almost despising,
Haply I think on thee, and then my state
(Like to the lark at break of day arising
From sullen earth) sings hymns at heaven's gate,
    For thy sweet love remembered such wealth brings,
    That then I scorn to change my state with kings.

WILLIAM SHAKESPEARE (1564–1616)

Her Anxiety

Earth in beauty dressed
Awaits returning spring.
All true love must die,
Alter at the best
Into some lesser thing.
Prove that I lie.

Such body lovers have,
Such exacting breath,
That they touch or sigh.
Every touch they give,
Love is nearer death.
Prove that I lie.

W. B. YEATS (1865–1939)

Lady 'Rogue' Singleton

Come, wed me, Lady Singleton,
And we will have a baby soon
And we will live in Edmonton
Where all the friendly people run.

I could never make you happy, darling,
Or give you the baby you want,
I would always very much rather, dear,
Live in a tent.

I am not a cold woman, Henry,
But I do not feel for you,
What I feel for the elephants and the miasmas
And the general view.

STEVIE SMITH (1902–71)

The Trees

The trees are coming into leaf
Like something almost being said;
The recent buds relax and spread,
Their greenness is a kind of grief.

Is it that they are born again
And we grow old? No, they die too.
Their yearly trick of looking new
Is written down in rings of grain.

Yet still the unresting castles thresh
In fullgrown thickness every May.
Last year is dead, they seem to say,
Begin afresh, afresh, afresh.

PHILIP LARKIN (1922–85)

Benediction

Thanks to the ear
that someone may hear

Thanks to seeing
that someone may see

Thanks to feeling
that someone may feel

Thanks to touch
that one may be touched

Thanks to flowering of white moon
and spreading shawl of black night
holding villages and cities together

JAMES BERRY (b. 1924)

The Sick Rose

O Rose thou art sick.
The invisible worm
That flies in the night
In the howling storm,

Has found out thy bed
Of crimson joy:
And his dark secret love
Does thy life destroy.

WILLIAM BLAKE (1757–1827)

'Much Madness is divinest Sense'

Much Madness is divinest Sense –
To a discerning Eye –
Much Sense – the starkest Madness –
'Tis the Majority
In this, as All, prevail –
Assent – and you are sane –
Demur – you're straightway dangerous –
And handled with a Chain –

EMILY DICKINSON (1830–86)

At Lord's

It is little I repair to the matches of the Southron folk,
   Though my own red roses there may blow;
It is little I repair to the matches of the Southron folk,
   Though the red roses crest the caps, I know.
For the field is full of shades as I near the shadowy coast,
And a ghostly batsman plays to the bowling of a ghost,
And I look through my tears on a soundless-clapping host
   As the run-stealers flicker to and fro,
      To and fro: –
O my Hornby and my Barlow long ago!

FRANCIS THOMPSON (1859–1907)

Rainforest

The forest drips and glows with green.
The tree-frog croaks his far-off song.
His voice is stillness, moss and rain
drunk from the forest ages long.

We cannot understand that call
unless we move into his dream,
where all is one and one is all
and frog and python are the same.

We with our quick dividing eyes
measure, distinguish and are gone.
The forest burns, the tree-frog dies,
yet one is all and all are one.

JUDITH WRIGHT (b. 1915)

Encounter at St. Martin's

I tell a wanderer's tale, the same
I began long ago, a boy in a barn,
I am always lost in it. The place
is always strange to me. In my pocket

the wrong money or none, the wrong paper,
maps of another town, the phrase book
for yesterday's language, just a ticket
to the next station, and my instructions.

In the lobby of the Banco Bilbao
a dark woman will slip me a key, a package,
the name of a hotel, a numbered account,
the first letters of an unknown alphabet.

KEN SMITH (b. 1938)

'Western wind when wilt thou blow'

Western wind when wilt thou blow
the small rain down can rain
Christ if my love were in my arms
and I in my bed again

ANON. (early 16th century)

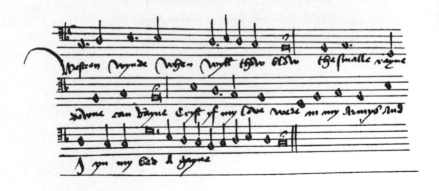

Westron wynde when wilt thou blow   Musical setting in a tenor part-book, dating from the early sixteenth century, which provides the only known source of this famous lyric. BL Royal MS, Appendix 58, f.5. By permission of The British Library Board.

Composed upon Westminster Bridge, September 3, 1802

Earth has not anything to show more fair:
Dull would he be of soul who could pass by
A sight so touching in its majesty:
This City now doth like a garment wear
The beauty of the morning; silent, bare,
Ships, towers, domes, theatres, and temples lie
Open unto the fields, and to the sky;
All bright and glittering in the smokeless air.
Never did sun more beautifully steep
In his first splendour valley, rock, or hill;
Ne'er saw I, never felt, a calm so deep!
The river glideth at his own sweet will:
Dear God! the very houses seem asleep;
And all that mighty heart is lying still!

WILLIAM WORDSWORTH (1770–1850)

Everyone Sang

Everyone suddenly burst out singing;
And I was filled with such delight
As prisoned birds must find in freedom,
Winging wildly across the white
Orchards and dark-green fields; on – on – and out of sight.

Everyone's voice was suddenly lifted;
And beauty came like the setting sun:
My heart was shaken with tears; and horror
Drifted away . . . O, but Everyone
Was a bird; and the song was wordless; the singing will never
    be done.

April 1919

SIEGFRIED SASSOON (1886–1967)

The Loch Ness Monster's Song

Sssnnnwhuffffll?
Hnwhuffl hhnnwfl hnfl hfl?
Gdroblboblhobngbl gbl gl g g g g glbgl.
Drublhaflablhaflubhafgabhaflhafl fl fl –
gm grawwwwww grf grawf awfgm graw gm.
Hovoplodok-doplodovok-plovodokot-doplodokosh?
Splgraw fok fok splgrafhatchgabrlgabrl fok splfok!
Zgra kra gka fok!
Grof grawff gahf?
Gombl mbl bl –
blm plm,
blm plm,
blm plm,
blp.

EDWIN MORGAN (b. 1920)

Living

The fire in leaf and grass
so green it seems
each summer the last summer.

The wind blowing, the leaves
shivering in the sun,
each day the last day.

A red salamander
so cold and so
easy to catch, dreamily

moves his delicate feet
and long tail. I hold
my hand open for him to go.

Each minute the last minute.

DENISE LEVERTOV (b. 1923)

Holy Sonnet

Death be not proud, though some have called thee
Mighty and dreadful, for thou art not so;
For those whom thou think'st thou dost overthrow
Die not, poor death, nor yet canst thou kill me.
From rest and sleep, which but thy pictures be,
Much pleasure, then from thee much more must flow;
And soonest our best men with thee do go,
Rest of their bones, and souls' delivery.
Thou art slave to Fate, chance, kings, and desperate men,
And dost with poison, war, and sickness dwell,
And poppy or charms can make us sleep as well,
And better than thy stroke; why swell'st thou then?
One short sleep past, we wake eternally,
And death shall be no more, Death thou shalt die.

JOHN DONNE (1572–1631)

'Trail all your pikes'

Trail all your pikes, dispirit every drum,
March in a slow procession from afar,
Ye silent, ye dejected men of war!
Be still the hautboys, and the flute be dumb!
Display no more, in vain, the lofty banner.
For see! where on the bier before ye lies
The pale, the fall'n, th'untimely sacrifice
To your mistaken shrine, to your false idol Honour!

from ALL IS VANITY

ANNE FINCH, Countess of Winchilsea (1661–1720)

Alas, Alack!

Ann, Ann!
  Come! quick as you can!
There's a fish that *talks*
  In the frying-pan.
Out of the fat,
  As clear as glass,
He put up his mouth
  And moaned 'Alas!'
Oh, most mournful,
  'Alas, alack!'
Then turned to his sizzling,
  And sank him back.

WALTER DE LA MARE (1873–1956)

Alas, Alack!   Drawing by W. Heath Robinson, © The Estate of
Mrs J. C. Robinson. By permission of Laurence Pollinger.

Immigrant

November '63: eight months in London.
I pause on the low bridge to watch the pelicans:
they float swanlike, arching their white necks
over only slightly ruffled bundles of wings,
burying awkward beaks in the lake's water.

I clench cold fists in my Marks and Spencer's jacket
and secretly test my accent once again:
St James's Park; St James's Park; St James's Park.

FLEUR ADCOCK (b. 1934)

I Am Becoming My Mother

Yellow/brown woman
fingers smelling always of onions

My mother raises rare blooms
and waters them with tea
her birth waters sang like rivers
my mother is now me

My mother had a linen dress
the colour of the sky
and stored lace and damask
tablecloths
to pull shame out of her eye.

I am becoming my mother
brown/yellow woman
fingers smelling always of onions.

LORNA GOODISON (b. 1947)

'Tagus farewell'

Tagus farewell, that westward with thy streams
Turns up the grains of gold already tried:
With spur and sail for I go seek the Thames
Gainward the sun that showeth her wealthy pride
And to the town which Brutus sought by dreams
Like bended moon doth lend her lusty side.
My king, my country, alone for whom I live,
Of mighty love the wings for this me give.

SIR THOMAS WYATT (1503–42)

'Tagus farewell' A rare example of a poem in the author's hand, in a handsome leatherbound notebook he kept from 1537 to 1542, which contains over one hundred poems by Wyatt and several by the Earl of Surrey, most of them in the hand of an amanuensis. The notebook was also used for drafts of letters and mathematical computations over a period of one hundred years. BL Egerton 2711, f.69. By permission of The British Library Board.

Snow

In the gloom of whiteness,
In the great silence of snow,
A child was sighing
And bitterly saying: 'Oh,
They have killed a white bird up there on her nest,
The down is fluttering from her breast!'
And still it fell through that dusky brightness
On the child crying for the bird of the snow.

EDWARD THOMAS (1878–1917)

Endymion Book 1st

A thing of beauty is a joy for ever:
Its loveliness increases; it will never
Pass into nothingness; but still will keep
A Bower quiet for us, and a sleep
Full of sweet dreams, and health, and quiet breathing
Therefore, on every morrow, are we wreathing
A flowery band to bind us to the earth,
Spite of Despondence, & of the inhuman dearth
Of noble natures, of the gloomy days,
Of all the unhealthy and oer-darkened ways
Made for our searching: yes, in spite of all
Some shape of beauty moves away the Pall
From our dark spirits. ~~and before us dawns~~
~~Like & after on th' [...] & Arthur's [...],~~

Endymion The opening lines of the autograph fair copy, with Keats's corrections.
MA 208. By permission of The Pierpont Morgan Library, New York.

Lines *from* Endymion

A thing of beauty is a joy for ever:
Its loveliness increases; it will never
Pass into nothingness; but still will keep
A bower quiet for us, and a sleep
Full of sweet dreams, and health, and quiet breathing.
Therefore, on every morrow, are we wreathing
A flowery band to bind us to the earth,
Spite of despondence, of the inhuman dearth
Of noble natures, of the gloomy days,
Of all the unhealthy and o'er-darkened ways
Made for our searching: yes, in spite of all,
Some shape of beauty moves away the pall
From our dark spirits.

JOHN KEATS (1795–1821)

Celia Celia

When I am sad and weary
When I think all hope has gone
When I walk along High Holborn
I think of you with nothing on

ADRIAN MITCHELL (b. 1932)

Goodbye

He breathed in air, he breathed out light.
Charlie Parker was my delight.

ADRIAN MITCHELL

Ragwort

They won't let railways alone, those yellow flowers.
They're that remorseless joy of dereliction
darkest banks exhale like vivid breath
as bricks divide to let them root between.
How every falling place concocts their smile,
taking what's left and making a song of it.

ANNE STEVENSON (b. 1933)

'The silver swan'

The silver swan, who living had no note,
When death approached unlocked her silent throat,
Leaning her breast against the reedy shore,
Thus sung her first and last, and sung no more:
Farewell all joys, O death come close mine eyes,
More geese than swans now live, more fools than wise.

ANON. (*c.* 1600)

The silver Swanne   A setting by the court composer Orlando Gibbons of
this anonymous elegiac poem, in *The First Set of Madrigals and Mottets* (1612).
It has been suggested that the poem may refer to the death of Edmund
Spenser, in 1599. BL Royal Mus. 15.e.2 (10). By permission of The British
Library Board.

'So we'll go no more a-roving'

So we'll go no more a-roving
   So late into the night,
Though the heart be still as loving,
   And the moon be still as bright.

For the sword outwears its sheath,
   And the soul wears out the breast,
And the heart must pause to breathe,
   And Love itself have rest.

Though the night was made for loving,
   And the day returns too soon,
Yet we'll go no more a-roving
   By the light of the moon.

GEORGE GORDON, LORD BYRON (1788–1824)

Teeth

English Teeth, English Teeth!
Shining in the sun
A part of British heritage
Aye, each and every one.

English Teeth, Happy Teeth!
Always having fun
Clamping down on bits of fish
And sausages half done.

English Teeth! HEROES' Teeth!
Hear them click! and clack!
Let's sing a song of praise to them –
Three Cheers for the Brown Grey and Black.

SPIKE MILLIGAN (b. 1918)

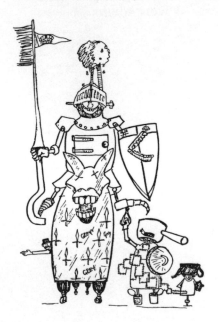

Teeth   Drawing by the author, in *Silly Verse for Kids* © Spike Milligan,
by permission of Spike Milligan Productions.

To My First White Hairs

Hirsute hell chimney-spouts, black thunderthroes
confluence of coarse cloudfleeces – my head sir! – scourbrush
in bitumen, past fossil beyond fingers of light – until . . .!

Sudden sprung as corn stalk after rain, watered milk weak;
as lightning shrunk to ant's antenna, shrivelled
off the febrile sight of crickets in the sun –

THREE WHITE HAIRS! frail invaders of the undergrowth
interpret time. I view them, wired wisps, vibrant coiled
beneath a magnifying glass, milk-thread presages

Of the hoary phase. Weave then, weave o quickly weave
your sham veneration. Knit me webs of winter sagehood,
nightcap, and the fungoid sequins of a crown.

WOLE SOYINKA (b. 1935)

Riddle-Me-Ree

My first is in life (not contained within heart)
My second's in whole but never in part.
My third's in forever, but also in vain.
My last's in ending, why not in pain?

is love the answer?

LIZ LOCHHEAD (b. 1947)

5 *At the Shops* **Tony Sarg** 1913

8 *Up River* **Tony Sarg** 1913

The Expulsion from Eden

In either hand the hast'ning angel caught
Our ling'ring parents, and to th' eastern gate
Led them direct, and down the cliff as fast
To the subjected plain; then disappeared.
They looking back, all th' eastern side beheld
Of Paradise, so late their happy seat,
Waved over by that flaming brand, the gate
With dreadful faces thronged and fiery arms:
Some natural tears they dropped, but wiped them soon;
The world was all before them, where to choose
Their place of rest, and Providence their guide:
They hand in hand with wand'ring steps and slow,
Through Eden took their solitary way.

from PARADISE LOST, BOOK XII

JOHN MILTON (1608–74)

'There was an Old Man with a beard'

There was an Old Man with a beard,
Who said, "It is just as I feared! –
Two Owls and a Hen,
Four Larks and a Wren,
Have all built their nests in my beard!"
from THE BOOK OF NONSENSE

EDWARD LEAR (1812–88)

There was an Old Man with a beard   Drawing by the author, from
The Book of Nonsense

Spring and Fall

to a young child

Margaret, are you grieving
Over Goldengrove unleaving?
Leaves, like the things of man, you
With your fresh thoughts care for, can you?
Ah! as the heart grows older
It will come to such sights colder
By and by, nor spare a sigh
Though worlds of wanwood leafmeal lie;
And yet you *will* weep and know why.
Now no matter, child, the name:
Sorrow's springs are the same.
Nor mouth had, no nor mind, expressed
What heart heard of, ghost guessed:
It is the blight man was born for,
It is Margaret you mourn for.

GERARD MANLEY HOPKINS (1844–89)

Dog Days

'When you stop to consider
The days spent dreaming of a future
And say then, that was my life.'

For the days are long –
From the first milk van
To the last shout in the night,
An eternity. But the weeks go by
Like birds; and the years, the years
Fly past anti-clockwise
Like clock hands in a bar mirror.

DEREK MAHON (b. 1941)

The Visitor

In Spanish he whispers there is no time left.
It is the sound of scythes arcing in wheat,
the ache of some field song in Salvador.
The wind along the prison, cautious
as Francisco's hands on the inside, touching
the walls as he walks, it is his wife's breath
slipping into his cell each night while he
imagines his hand to be hers. It is a small country.

There is nothing one man will not do to another.

CAROLYN FORCHÉ (b. 1950)

Ariel's Song

Full fathom five thy father lies,
   Of his bones are coral made:
Those are pearls that were his eyes,
   Nothing of him that doth fade,
But doth suffer a sea-change
Into something rich, and strange:
Sea-nymphs hourly ring his knell –
Hark! now I hear them,
   Ding-dong bell.
from THE TEMPEST

WILLIAM SHAKESPEARE (1564–1616)

Meeting at Night

The grey sea and the long black land;
And the yellow half-moon large and low;
And the startled little waves that leap
In fiery ringlets from their sleep,
As I gain the cove with pushing prow,
And quench its speed i' the slushy sand.

Then a mile of warm sea-scented beach;
Three fields to cross till a farm appears;
A tap at the pane, the quick sharp scratch
And blue spurt of a lighted match,
And a voice less loud, thro' its joys and fears,
Than the two hearts beating each to each!

ROBERT BROWNING (1812–89)

Prelude I

The winter evening settles down
With smell of steaks in passageways.
Six o'clock.
The burnt-out ends of smoky days.
And now a gusty shower wraps
The grimy scraps
Of withered leaves about your feet
And newspapers from vacant lots;
The showers beat
On broken blinds and chimney-pots,
And at the corner of the street
A lonely cab-horse steams and stamps.

And then the lighting of the lamps.

T. S. ELIOT (1888–1965)

London Airport

Last night in London Airport
I saw a wooden bin
labelled UNWANTED LITERATURE
IS TO BE PLACED HEREIN.
So I wrote a poem
and popped it in.

CHRISTOPHER LOGUE (b. 1926)

Taid's Grave

Rain on lilac leaves. In the dusk
they show me the grave,
a casket of stars underfoot,
his name there, and his language.

Voice of thrushes in rain.
My cousin Gwynfor eases me
into the green cave.
Wet hands of lilac

touch my wrist and the secret
unfreckled underside of my arm
daring fingers to count
five warm blue eggs.

GILLIAN CLARKE (b. 1937)

Taid: Welsh for grandfather.

The Coming of Grendel

Now from the marshlands under the mist-mountains
Came Grendel prowling; branded with God's ire.
This murderous monster was minded to entrap
Some hapless human in that high hall.
On he came under the clouds, until clearly
He could see the great golden feasting place,
Glimmering wine-hall of men. Not his first
Raid was this on the homeplace of Hrothgar.
Never before though and never afterward
Did he encounter hardier defenders of a hall.

from BEOWULF

translated by GERARD BENSON

In my Craft or Sullen Art

In my craft or sullen art
Exercised in the still night
When only the moon rages
And the lovers lie abed
With all their griefs in their arms,
I labour by singing light
Not for ambition or bread
Or the strut and trade of charms
On the ivory stages
But for the common wages
Of their most secret heart.

Not for the proud man apart
From the raging moon I write
On these spindrift pages
Nor for the towering dead
With their nightingales and psalms
But for the lovers, their arms
Round the griefs of the ages,
Who pay no praise or wages
Nor heed my craft or art.

DYLAN THOMAS (1914–53)

Midsummer, Tobago

Broad sun-stoned beaches.

White heat.
A green river.

A bridge,
scorched yellow palms

from the summer-sleeping house
drowsing through August.

Days I have held,
days I have lost,

days that outgrow, like daughters,
my harbouring arms.

DEREK WALCOTT (b. 1930)

XLIII

How do I love thee? Let me count the ways.
I love thee to the depth and breadth and height
My soul can reach, when feeling out of sight
For the ends of Being and ideal Grace.
I love thee to the level of everyday's
Most quiet need, by sun and candle-light.
I love thee freely, as men strive for Right;
I love thee purely, as they turn from Praise.
I love thee with the passion put to use
In my old griefs; and with my childhood's faith.
I love thee with the love I seemed to lose
With my lost Saints! — I love thee with the breath,
Smiles, tears, of all my life — and, if God choose,
I shall but love thee better after death.

How do I love thee? Autograph manuscript, with corrections, of one of the most popular 'Sonnets from the Portuguese'. BL Add. MS 43487, f.49. By permission of The British Library Board.

Sonnet from the Portuguese

How do I love thee? Let me count the ways.
I love thee to the depth and breadth and height
My soul can reach, when feeling out of sight
For the ends of Being and ideal Grace.
I love thee to the level of everyday's
Most quiet need, by sun and candlelight.
I love thee freely, as men strive for Right;
I love thee purely, as they turn from Praise.
I love thee with the passion put to use
In my old griefs, and with my childhood's faith.
I love thee with a love I seemed to lose
With my lost saints, – I love thee with the breath,
Smiles, tears, of all my life! – and, if God choose,
I shall but love thee better after death.

ELIZABETH BARRETT BROWNING (1806–61)

Handbag

My mother's old leather handbag,
crowded with letters she carried
all through the war. The smell
of my mother's handbag: mints
and lipstick and Coty powder.
The look of those letters, softened
and worn at the edges, opened,
read, and refolded so often.
Letters from my father. Odour
of leather and powder, which ever
since then has meant womanliness,
and love, and anguish, and war.

RUTH FAINLIGHT (b. 1931)

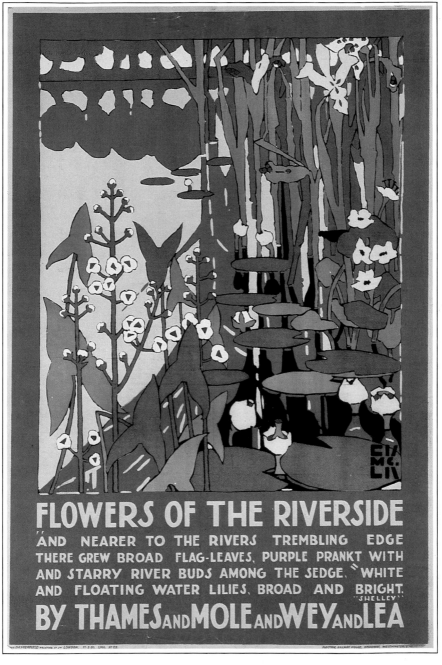

9 *Flowers of the Riverside* **E. McKnight Kauffer** 1920

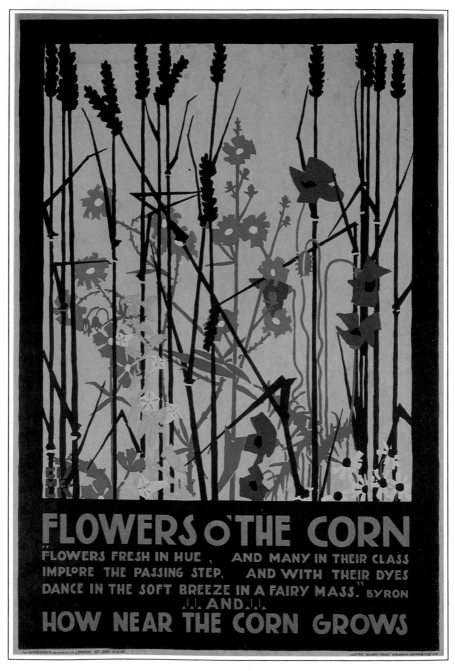

10 *Flowers of the Corn* **E. McKnight Kauffer** 1920

11 *Blue Bells, Kew Gardens* **E. McKnight Kauffer** 1920

12 *The Forest Glades of Epping* **E. McKnight Kauffer** 1920

Symphony in Yellow

An omnibus across the bridge
   Crawls like a yellow butterfly,
   And, here and there, a passer-by
Shows like a little restless midge.

Big barges full of yellow hay
   Are moored against the shadowy wharf,
   And, like a yellow silken scarf,
The thick fog hangs along the quay.

The yellow leaves begin to fade
   And flutter from the Temple elms,
   And at my feet the pale green Thames
Lies like a rod of rippled jade.

OSCAR WILDE (1854–1900)

Caricature of Oscar Wilde
in a Top Hat. Black and white
drawing by Beatrice Whistler.
Birnie Philip Bequest. By
permission of The Hunterian
Art Gallery, University of
Glasgow.

'Sumer is icumen in' English and Latin texts, with music, of the earliest known English round. The Latin text is completely unrelated to the English original. From a manuscript transcribed at Reading Abbey in the early thirteenth century. BL Harley 978, f.11v. By permission of The British Library Board.

'Sumer is icumen in'

Sumer is icumen in,
Loud sing cuckoo!
Groweth seed and bloweth mead
And springeth the wood now.
Sing cuckoo!

Ewe bleateth after lamb,
Cow loweth after calf,
Bullock starteth, buck farteth,
Merry sing cuckoo!

Cuckoo, cuckoo!
Well singest thou cuckoo,
Nor cease thou never now!

Sing cuckoo now, sing cuckoo!
Sing cuckoo, sing cuckoo now!

ANON. (13th century)

Song

Stop all the clocks, cut off the telephone,
Prevent the dog from barking with a juicy bone,
Silence the pianos and with muffled drum
Bring out the coffin, let the mourners come.

Let aeroplanes circle moaning overhead
Scribbling on the sky the message He Is Dead,
Put crêpe bows round the white necks of the public doves,
Let the traffic policemen wear black cotton gloves.

He was my North, my South, my East and West,
My working week and my Sunday rest,
My noon, my midnight, my talk, my song;
I thought that love would last for ever: I was wrong.

The stars are not wanted now; put out every one,
Pack up the moon and dismantle the sun,
Pour away the ocean and sweep up the wood;
For nothing now can ever come to any good.

W. H. AUDEN (1907–73)

80

The Ancients of the World

The salmon lying in the depths of Llyn Llifon,
   Secretly as a thought in a dark mind,
Is not so old as the owl of Cwm Cowlyd
   Who tells her sorrow nightly on the wind.

The ousel singing in the woods of Cilgwri,
   Tirelessly as a stream over the mossed stones,
Is not so old as the toad of Cors Fochno
   Who feels the cold skin sagging round his bones.

The toad and the ousel and the stag of Rhedynfre,
   That has cropped each leaf from the tree of life,
Are not so old as the owl of Cwm Cowlyd,
   That the proud eagle would have to wife.

R. S. THOMAS (b. 1913)

Day Trip

Two women, seventies, hold hands
on the edge of Essex,
hair in strong nets,
shrieked laughter echoing gulls
as shingle sucks from under feet
easing in brine.

There must be an unspoken point
when the sea feels like
their future. No longer paddling,
ankles submerge in lace,
in satin ripple.
Dress hems darken.

They do not risk their balance
for the shimmering of ships
at the horizon's sweep
as, thigh deep, they inch on
fingers splayed, wrists bent,
learning to walk again.

CAROLE SATYAMURTI (b. 1939)

In Time of 'The Breaking of Nations'

I

Only a man harrowing clods
   In a slow silent walk
With an old horse that stumbles and nods
   Half asleep as they stalk.

II

Only thin smoke without flame
   From the heaps of couch-grass;
Yet this will go onward the same
   Though Dynasties pass.

III

Yonder a maid and her wight
   Come whispering by:
War's annals will cloud into night
   Ere their story die.

THOMAS HARDY (1840–1928)

'Thou art my battle axe and weapons of war: for with thee will I break in
pieces the nations, and with thee will I destroy kingdoms' (Jeremiah: 51.20).

London Bells

Two sticks and an apple,
Ring the bells at Whitechapel.

Old Father Bald Pate,
Ring the bells Aldgate.

Maids in white aprons,
Ring the bells at St. Catherine's.

Oranges and lemons,
Ring the bells at St. Clement's.

When will you pay me?
Ring the bells at the Old Bailey.

When I am rich,
Ring the bells at Fleetditch.

When will that be?
Ring the bells at Stepney.

When I am old,
Ring the great bell at Paul's.

ANON. (early 18th century)

London Bells.

Two Sticks & and Apple,
Ring ỹ Bells at Whitechapple
Old Father Bald Pate,
Ring ỹ Bells Aldgate,
Maids in white Aprons,
Ring ỹ Bells ɔ St Cathrines,
　　　　　Oranges

Oranges and Lemmons,
Ring ỹ Bells at St Clemens,
When will you pay me,
Ring ỹ Bells at ỹ Old Bailey,
When I am Rich,
Ring ỹ Bells at Fleet ditch,
When will that be,
Ring ỹ Bells at Stepney,
When I am Old,
Ring ỹ great Bell at Pauls.

London Bells　The traditional London rhyme as it appears in an early hand-set printed children's book, *Tommy Thumb's Pretty Song Book* (1744), Vol. II. By permission of The British Library Board.

The Tyger A much-corrected autograph draft of the poem, in Blake's notebook, the 'Rossetti Manuscript'. BL Add. MS 49460, f.56. By permission of The British Library Board .

The Tyger

Tyger Tyger, burning bright,
In the forests of the night;
What immortal hand or eye,
Could frame thy fearful symmetry?

In what distant deeps or skies
Burnt the fire of thine eyes!
On what wings dare he aspire?
What the hand, dare sieze the fire?

And what shoulder, & what art,
Could twist the sinews of thy heart?
And when thy heart began to beat,
What dread hand? & what dread feet?

What the hammer? what the chain?
In what furnace was thy brain?
What the anvil? what dread grasp,
Dare its deadly terrors clasp?

When the stars threw down their spears
And water'd heaven with their tears:
Did he smile his work to see?
Did he who made the Lamb make thee?

Tyger Tyger, burning bright,
In the forests of the night:
What immortal hand or eye,
Dare frame thy fearful symmetry?

WILLIAM BLAKE (1757–1827)

Delay

The radiance of that star that leans on me
Was shining years ago. The light that now
Glitters up there my eye may never see,
And so the time lag teases me with how

Love that loves now may not reach me until
Its first desire is spent. The star's impulse
Must wait for eyes to claim it beautiful
And love arrived may find us somewhere else.

ELIZABETH JENNINGS (b. 1926)

Everything Changes

after Brecht, *'Alles wandelt sich'*

Everything changes. We plant
trees for those born later
but what's happened has happened,
and poisons poured into the seas
cannot be drained out again.

What's happened has happened.
Poisons poured into the seas
cannot be drained out again, but
everything changes. We plant
trees for those born later.

CICELY HERBERT (b. 1937)

Roundel

Now welcome Summer with thy sunnė soft,
That hast this winter's weathers overshake,
And driven away the longė nightės black.

Saint Valentine, that art full high aloft,
Thus singen smallė fowlės for thy sake:
Now welcome Summer with thy sunnė soft,
That hast this winter's weathers overshake.

Well have they cause for to gladden oft,
Since each of them recovered hath his make.
Full blissful may they singė when they wake:
Now welcome Summer with thy sunnė soft,
That hast this winter's weathers overshake,
And driven away the longė nightės black!

from THE PARLIAMENT OF FOWLS

GEOFFREY CHAUCER (1340?–1400)

Introduction to *The Parliament of Fowls* from a fifteenth-century copy of
Chaucer's Works in the Cambridge University Library. GG.4.27, f.480b. By
permission of the Syndics of Cambridge University Library.

Dreams

Here we are all, by day; by night we're hurled
By dreams, each one, into a several world.

ROBERT HERRICK (1591–1674)

Sonnet

What lips my lips have kissed, and where, and why,
I have forgotten, and what arms have lain
Under my head till morning; but the rain
Is full of ghosts tonight, that tap and sigh
Upon the glass and listen for reply,
And in my heart there stirs a quiet pain
For unremembered lads that not again
Will turn to me at midnight with a cry.
Thus in the winter stands the lonely tree,
Nor knows what birds have vanished one by one,
Yet knows its boughs more silent than before:
I cannot say what loves have come and gone,
I only know that summer sang in me
A little while, that in me sings no more.

EDNA ST. VINCENT MILLAY (1892–1950)

13 *Essex* **C. R. W. Nevinson** 1924

16 *Kent* **C. R. W. Nevinson** 1924

And Yet the Books

And yet the books will be there on the shelves, separate beings,
That appeared once, still wet
As shining chestnuts under a tree in autumn,
And, touched, coddled, began to live
In spite of fires on the horizon, castles blown up,
Tribes on the march, planets in motion.
"We are," they said, even as their pages
Were being torn out, or a buzzing flame
Licked away their letters. So much more durable
Than we are, whose frail warmth
Cools down with memory, disperses, perishes.
I imagine the earth when I am no more:
Nothing happens, no loss, it's still a strange pageant,
Women's dresses, dewy lilacs, a song in the valley.
Yet the books will be there on the shelves, well born,
Derived from people, but also from radiance, heights.

CZESLAW MILOSZ (b. 1911)
translated by CZESLAW MILOSZ AND ROBERT HASS

The Leader

I wanna be the leader
I wanna be the leader
Can I be the leader?
Can I? I can?
Promise? Promise?
Yippee, I'm the leader
I'm the leader

OK what shall we do?

ROGER McGOUGH (b. 1937)

from To the City of London

Above all rivers thy river hath renown,
Whose beryl streamès, pleasant and preclare,
Under thy lusty wallès runneth down;
Where many a swan doth swim with wingès fair,
Where many a barge doth sail, and row with oar,
Where many a ship doth rest with top-royal.
O town of townès, patron and not compare,
London, thou art the flower of Cities all.

WILLIAM DUNBAR (1465?–1530?)

To the City of London   The 'river' stanza. The full text of the poem is
copied into *The Chronicle of London 1215–1509*, where the poem is said to have
been 'made' while the company was sitting at dinner. BL Cotton MS Vitell.
A.XVI, f.200v. By permission of The British Library Board.

On First Looking into Chapman's Homer

Much have I travell'd in the realms of gold,
   And many goodly states and kingdoms seen;
   Round many western islands have I been
Which bards in fealty to Apollo hold.
Oft of one wide expanse had I been told
   That deep-brow'd Homer ruled as his demesne;
   Yet did I never breathe its pure serene
Till I heard Chapman speak out loud and bold:
Then felt I like some watcher of the skies
   When a new planet swims into his ken;
Or like stout Cortez when with eagle eyes
   He star'd at the Pacific – and all his men
Look'd at each other with a wild surmise –
   Silent, upon a peak in Darien.

JOHN KEATS (1795–1821)

A Dead Statesman

I could not dig: I dared not rob:
Therefore I lied to please the mob.
Now all my lies are proved untrue
And I must face the men I slew.
What tale shall serve me here among
Mine angry and defrauded young?

from EPITAPHS OF THE WAR 1914–18

RUDYARD KIPLING (1865–1936)

Modern Secrets

Last night I dreamt in Chinese.
Eating Yankee shredded wheat
I said it in English
To a friend who answered
In monosyllables:
All of which I understood.

The dream shrank to its fiction.
I had understood its end
Many years ago. The sallow child
Ate rice from its ricebowl
And hides still in the cupboard
With the china and tea-leaves.

SHIRLEY GEOK-LIN LIM (b. 1944)

Sergeant Brown's Parrot

Many policemen wear upon their shoulders
Cunning little radios. To pass away the time
They talk about the traffic to them, listen to the news,
And it helps them to Keep Down Crime.

But Sergeant Brown, he wears upon his shoulder
A tall green parrot as he's walking up and down
And all the parrot says is ''Who's-a-pretty-boy-then?''
''I am,'' says Sergeant Brown.

KIT WRIGHT (b. 1944)

Sergeant Brown's Parrot Drawing by Posy Simmonds, © Posy
Simmonds. By permission of Collins Publishers.

'I have a gentil cock'

I have a gentil cock
    croweth me day
he doth me risen early
    my matins for to say

I have a gentil cock
    comen he is of great
his comb is of red coral
    his tail is of jet

I have a gentil cock
    comen he is of kind
his comb is of red sorrel
    his tail is of inde

his legs be of azure
    so gentil and so small
his spurs are of silver white
    into the wortewale

his eyes are of crystal
    locked all in amber
and every night he percheth him
    in my lady's chamber

ANON. (early 15th century)

What Am I After All

What am I after all but a child, pleas'd with the sound of
    my own name? repeating it over and over;
I stand apart to hear – it never tires me.

To you your name also;
Did you think there was nothing but two or three
    pronunciations in the sound of your name?

WALT WHITMAN (1819–92)

Piano

Softly, in the dusk, a woman is singing to me;
Taking me back down the vista of years, till I see
A child sitting under the piano, in the boom of the tingling
  strings
And pressing the small, poised feet of a mother who smiles as
  she sings.

In spite of myself, the insidious mastery of song
Betrays me back, till the heart of me weeps to belong
To the old Sunday evenings at home, with winter outside
And hymns in the cosy parlour, the tinkling piano our guide.

So now it is vain for the singer to burst into clamour
With the great black piano appassionato. The glamour
Of childish days is upon me, my manhood is cast
Down in the flood of remembrance, I weep like a child for the
  past.

D. H. LAWRENCE (1885–1930)

Mmenson

Summon now the kings of the forest,
horn of the elephant,
mournful call of the elephant;

summon the emirs, kings of the desert,
horses caparisoned, beaten gold bent,
archers and criers, porcupine arrows, bows bent;

recount now the gains and the losses:
Agades, Sokoto, El Hassan dead in his tent,
the silks and the brasses, the slow weary tent

of our journeys down slopes, dry river courses;
land of the lion, land of the leopard, elephant
country; tall grasses, thick prickly herbs. Blow elephant

trumpet; summon the horses,
dead horses, our losses: the bent
slow bow of the Congo, the watering Niger . . .

EDWARD KAMAU BRATHWAITE (b. 1930)

Light

I live for books
and light to read them in.
                              Waterlilies
reaching up
from the depths of the pond
algae dark,
the frog loves a jell of
blue-green water,
                        the bud
scales
a rope of stem,
then floats in sunshine. Like soap
in the morning bath.
This book I read
floats in my hand like a waterlily
coming out of the nutrient waters
of thought
and light shines on us both,
the morning's breviary.

DIANE WAKOSKI (b. 1937)

from The Song of Solomon

My beloved spake, and said unto me, Rise up, my love, my fair
    one, and come away.
For lo, the winter is past, the rain is over, and gone.
The flowers appear on the earth, the time of the singing of
    birds is come, and the voice of the turtle is heard in our
    land.
The fig tree putteth forth her green figs, and the vines with
    the tender grape give a good smell.
Arise, my love, my fair one, and come away.

THE KING JAMES BIBLE (1611)

'You took away all the oceans and all the room'

You took away all the oceans and all the room.
You gave me my shoe-size in earth with bars around it.
Where did it get you? Nowhere.
You left me my lips, and they shape words, even in silence.

OSIP MANDELSTAM (1891–1938)

translated by CLARENCE BROWN AND W. S. MERWIN

Wet Evening in April

The birds sang in the wet trees
And as I listened to them it was a hundred years from now
And I was dead and someone else was listening to them.
But I was glad I had recorded for him
  The melancholy.

PATRICK KAVANAGH (1906–67)

I Saw a Jolly Hunter

I saw a jolly hunter
With a jolly gun
Walking in the country
In the jolly sun.

In the jolly meadow
Sat a jolly hare.
Saw the jolly hunter.
Took jolly care.

Hunter jolly eager –
Sight of jolly prey.
Forgot gun pointing
Wrong jolly way.

Jolly hunter jolly head
Over heels gone.
Jolly old safety catch
Not jolly on.

Bang went the jolly gun.
Hunter jolly dead.
Jolly hare got clean away.
Jolly good, I said.

CHARLES CAUSLEY (b. 1917)

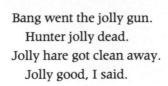

I Saw a Jolly Hunter   Drawing by
Pat Marriott, from *Figgie Hobbin*.
By permission of Macmillan London.

Aunt Jennifer's Tigers

Aunt Jennifer's tigers prance across a screen,
Bright topaz denizens of a world of green.
They do not fear the men beneath the tree;
They pace in sleek chivalric certainty.

Aunt Jennifer's fingers fluttering through her wool
Find even the ivory needle hard to pull.
The massive weight of Uncle's wedding band
Sits heavily upon Aunt Jennifer's hand.

When Aunt is dead, her terrified hands will lie
Still ringed with ordeals she was mastered by.
The tigers in the panel that she made
Will go on prancing, proud and unafraid.

ADRIENNE RICH (b. 1929)

Old English Riddle

A moth, I thought, munching a word.
How marvellously weird! a worm
Digesting a man's sayings –
A sneakthief nibbling in the shadows
At the shape of a poet's thunderous phrases –
How unutterably strange!
And the pilfering parasite none the wiser
For the words he has swallowed.

from THE EXETER BOOK
translated by GERARD BENSON

Answer: Bookworm

Ⓜ oððe poꞃo ꝼꞃæꞇ mebæꞇ þuhꞇæ ꝑꞃæꞇ·lıcu
ꝑꞃꞃo þuıc þæꞇ punꝌoꞃ ꞅꞃ ꝼꞃuꞇ͛ꞃn þæꞇ ꝛe ꝑꞃꞃum ꝼoꞃı
ꞅꞃæꞇꞁꞎ ꝑꞇꞕ ꞅꞃeꝌ ꞃumꞁ͛ þꞇbꝼ lıþyꞃꞇꞃo þꞃꞃm ꝼæ͛ꞇꞃ·ꞇꞃꞃꞎ
cꞃꞇꝌ͛ ꞁþꞇꞁ ꝼꞁꞃꞎꞃꞃꞃn ꝼꞇꞅbol ꝼꞃl ꞃꞎꞁꞎꞇ neꝑꞇꞁ ꝑꞎꞇꞇꞃ

Old English Riddle from *The Exeter Book*, a manuscript of about the year 1000,
containing over ninety riddles and several other Old English poems. Reprinted
with the permission of the Dean and Chapter of Exeter Cathedral.

Virtue

Sweet day, so cool, so calm, so bright,
The bridal of the earth and sky:
The dew shall weep thy fall tonight;
                      For thou must die.

Sweet rose, whose hue angry and brave
Bids the rash gazer wipe his eye:
Thy root is ever in its grave,
                      And thou must die.

Sweet spring, full of sweet days and roses,
A box where sweets compacted lie;
My music shows ye have your closes,
                      And all must die.

Only a sweet and virtuous soul,
Like seasoned timber, never gives;
But though the whole world turn to coal,
                      Then chiefly lives.

GEORGE HERBERT (1593–1633)

'I know the truth – give up all other truths!'

I know the truth – give up all other truths!
No need for people anywhere on earth to struggle.
Look – it is evening, look, it is nearly night:
what do you speak of, poets, lovers, generals?

The wind is level now, the earth is wet with dew,
the storm of stars in the sky will turn to quiet.
And soon all of us will sleep under the earth, we
who never let each other sleep above it.

1915

MARINA TSVETAYEVA (1892–1941)
translated by ELAINE FEINSTEIN

Love Without Hope

Love without hope, as when the young bird-catcher
Swept off his tall hat to the Squire's own daughter,
So let the imprisoned larks escape and fly
Singing about her head, as she rode by.

ROBERT GRAVES (1895–1985)

Full Moon and Little Frieda

A cool small evening shrunk to a dog bark and the clank
                              of a bucket –

And you listening.
A spider's web, tense for the dew's touch.
A pail lifted, still and brimming – mirror
To tempt a first star to a tremor.

Cows are going home in the lane there, looping the hedges
                       with their warm wreaths of breath –
A dark river of blood, many boulders,
Balancing unspilled milk.

'Moon!' you cry suddenly, 'Moon! Moon!'

The moon has stepped back like an artist gazing amazed
                              at a work
That points at him amazed.

TED HUGHES (b. 1930)

'Since there's no help, come let us kiss and part'

Since there's no help, come let us kiss and part,
Nay, I have done: you get no more of me,
And I am glad, yea glad with all my heart
That thus so cleanly I myself can free,
Shake hands forever, cancel all our vows,
And when we meet at any time again,
Be it not seen in either of our brows
That we one jot of former love retain.
Now at the last gasp of love's latest breath,
When his pulse failing, passion speechless lies,
When faith is kneeling by his bed of death,
And innocence is closing up his eyes,
    Now if thou wouldst, when all have given him over,
    From death to life thou mightst him yet recover.

MICHAEL DRAYTON (1563–1631)

'Into my heart an air that kills'

Into my heart an air that kills
   From yon far country blows:
What are those blue remembered hills,
   What spires, what farms are those?

That is the land of lost content,
   I see it shining plain,
The happy highways where I went
   And cannot come again.

from A SHROPSHIRE LAD

A. E. HOUSMAN (1859–1936)

Dolor

I have known the inexorable sadness of pencils,
Neat in their boxes, dolor of pad and paper-weight,
All the misery of manilla folders and mucilage,
Desolation in immaculate public places,
Lonely reception room, lavatory, switchboard,
The unalterable pathos of basin and pitcher,
Ritual of multigraph, paper-clip, comma,
Endless duplication of lives and objects.
And I have seen dust from the walls of institutions,
Finer than flour, alive, more dangerous than silica,
Sift, almost invisible, through long afternoons of tedium,
Dropping a fine film on nails and delicate eyebrows,
Glazing the pale hair, the duplicate grey standard faces.

THEODORE ROETHKE (1908–63)

The Cries of London

Here's fine rosemary, sage, and thyme.
Come buy my ground ivy.
Here's fetherfew, gilliflowers and rue.
Come buy my knotted marjorum, ho!
Come buy my mint, my fine green mint.
Here's fine lavender for your cloaths.
Here's parsley and winter-savory,
And hearts-ease, which all do choose.
Here's balm and hissop, and cinquefoil,
All fine herbs, it is well known.
    Let none despise the merry, merry cries
    Of famous London-town!

Here's fine herrings, eight a groat.
Hot codlins, pies and tarts.
New mackerel! have to sell.
Come buy my Wellfleet oysters, ho!
Come buy my whitings fine and new.
Wives, shall I mend your husbands horns?
I'll grind your knives to please your wives,
And very nicely cut your corns.
Maids, have you any hair to sell,
Either flaxen, black, or brown?
    Let none despise the merry, merry cries
    Of famous London-town!

ANON. (17th century)

The Cries of London   A setting by Orlando Gibbons of several London
'Cries' for five singers and five viol players. BL. Add.MS 29373, f.33v. By
permission of The British Library Board.

ALTVS. Pars 2.

64.

Good sausage

New oysters new, new plaise new   new

mackerell new,

Ha' ye any kirchmstuffe maydes.

Ha ye any kirchmstuffe maydes

I ha' ripe cowcumbers ripe

Salt, salt, salt to barge to, Hard onyons hard, Al' a black

A 14-Year-Old Convalescent Cat in the Winter

I want him to have another living summer,
to lie in the sun and enjoy the *douceur de vivre* –
because the sun, like golden rum in a rummer,
is what makes an idle cat *un tout petit peu ivre* –

I want him to lie stretched out, contented,
revelling in the heat, his fur all dry and warm,
an Old Age Pensioner, retired, resented
by no one, and happinesses in a beelike swarm

to settle on him – postponed for another season
that last fated hateful journey to the vet
from which there is no return (and age the reason),
which must soon come – as I cannot forget.

GAVIN EWART (b. 1916)

Come. And Be My Baby

The highway is full of big cars
going nowhere fast
And folks is smoking anything that'll burn
Some people wrap their lives around a cocktail glass
And you sit wondering
where you're going to turn.
I got it.
Come. And be my baby.

Some prophets say the world is gonna end tomorrow
But others say we've got a week or two
The paper is full of every kind of blooming horror
And you sit wondering
what you're gonna do.
I got it.
Come. And be my baby.

MAYA ANGELOU (b. 1928)

'Ich am of Irlonde'

I am of Ireland,
And of the holy land
Of Ireland.

Good sir, pray I thee,
For of saint charity,
Come and dance with me
In Ireland.

ANON. (14th century)

Song

Now sleeps the crimson petal, now the white;
Nor waves the cypress in the palace walk;
Nor winks the gold fin in the porphyry font:
The fire-fly wakens: waken thou with me.

Now droops the milkwhite peacock like a ghost,
And like a ghost she glimmers on to me.

Now lies the Earth all Danaë to the stars,
And all thy heart lies open unto me.

Now slides the silent meteor on, and leaves
A shining furrow, as thy thoughts in me.

Now folds the lily all her sweetness up,
And slips into the bosom of the lake:
So fold thyself, my dearest, thou, and slip
Into my bosom and be lost in me.

from THE PRINCESS

ALFRED, LORD TENNYSON (1809–92)

The Embankment

(*The Fantasia of a Fallen Gentleman on a Cold, Bitter Night*)

Once, in finesse of fiddles found I ecstasy,
In a flash of gold heels on the hard pavement.
Now see I
That warmth's the very stuff of poesy.
Oh, God, make small
The old star-eaten blanket of the sky,
That I may fold it round me and in comfort lie.

T. E. HULME (1883–1917)

THE PROUD CITY

A NEW VIEW OF ST. PAUL'S CATHEDRAL FROM BREAD STREET

"...the principal Ornament of our royal City,
to the Honour of our Government, and
of this our Realm...."

Letters Patent under the Great Seal of England the 12th day Nov. 1673.

17 *St. Paul's* **Walter Spradbery** 1944

THE PROUD CITY

THE NOBLE FABRIC OF THE CHURCH OF ST. CLEMENT DANES

"Where the fair columns of St. Clement stand
Whose straiten'd bounds encroach upon
the Strand;"

John Gay

18 *St. Clement Danes* **Walter Spradbery** 1944

THE PROUD CITY

THE TEMPLE CHURCH AND LIBRARY AFTER BOMBARDMENT

"So may the Winged Horse, your ancient badge and cognisance, still flourish!"

Charles Lamb

19 *Temple Church and Library* **Walter Spradbery** 1944

THE PROUD CITY

CHELSEA POWER HOUSE FROM MEEK STREET

" the poor buildings lose themselves in the dim sky, and the tall chimneys become campanili, and the warehouses are palaces in the night. and the whole city hangs in the heavens..."

James McNeill Whistler

20 *Chelsea Power House* **Walter Spradbery** 1944

Stars and planets

Trees are cages for them: water holds its breath
To balance them without smudging on its delicate meniscus.
Children watch them playing in their heavenly playground;
Men use them to lug ships across oceans, through firths.

They seem so twinkle-still, but they never cease
Inventing new spaces and huge explosions
And migrating in mathematical tribes over
The steppes of space at their outrageous ease.

It's hard to think that the earth is one –
This poor sad bearer of wars and disasters
Rolls-Roycing round the sun with its load of gangsters,
Attended only by the loveless moon.

NORMAN MacCAIG (b. 1910)

The Uncertainty of the Poet

I am a poet.
I am very fond of bananas.

I am bananas.
I am very fond of a poet.

I am a poet of bananas.
I am very fond.

A fond poet of 'I am, I am' –
Very bananas.

Fond of 'Am I bananas?
Am I?' – a very poet.

Bananas of a poet!
Am I fond? Am I very?

Poet bananas! I am.
I am fond of a 'very'.

I am of very fond bananas.
Am I a poet?

WENDY COPE (b. 1945)

'I saw a Peacock with a fiery tail'

I saw a Peacock with a fiery tail
I saw a blazing Comet drop down hail
I saw a Cloud with Ivy circled round
I saw a sturdy Oak creep on the ground
I saw a Pismire swallow up a Whale
I saw a raging Sea brim full of Ale
I saw a Venice Glass sixteen foot deep
I saw a Well full of men's tears that weep
I saw their Eyes all in a flame of fire
I saw a House as big as the Moon and higher
I saw the Sun even in the midst of night
I saw the Man that saw this wondrous sight.

ANON. (17th century)

from **Frost at Midnight**

The Frost performs its secret ministry,
Unhelped by any wind. The owlet's cry
Came loud – and hark, again! loud as before.
The inmates of my cottage, all at rest,
Have left me to that solitude, which suits
Abstruser musings: save that at my side
My cradled infant slumbers peacefully.
'Tis calm indeed! so calm, that it disturbs
And vexes meditation with its strange
And extreme silentness. Sea, hill, and wood,
This populous village! Sea, and hill, and wood,
With all the numberless goings-on of life,
Inaudible as dreams!

SAMUEL TAYLOR COLERIDGE (1772–1834)

Snow

The room was suddenly rich and the great bay-window was
Spawning snow and pink roses against it
Soundlessly collateral and incompatible:
World is suddener than we fancy it.

World is crazier and more of it than we think,
Incorrigibly plural. I peel and portion
A tangerine and spit the pips and feel
The drunkenness of things being various.

And the fire flames with a bubbling sound for world
Is more spiteful and gay than one supposes –
On the tongue on the eyes on the ears in the palms of one's
    hands –
There is more than glass between the snow and the huge
    roses.

LOUIS MacNEICE (1907–63)

On Himself

Abstracted by silence from the age of seven,
Deafened and penned by as black calamity
As twice to be born, I cannot without pity
Contemplate myself as an infant;

Or fail to speak of silence as a priestess
Calling to serve in the temple of a skull
Her innocent choice. It is barely possible
Not to be affected by such a distress.

DAVID WRIGHT (b. 1920)

Sometimes

Sometimes things don't go, after all,
from bad to worse. Some years, muscadel
faces down frost; green thrives; the crops don't fail,
sometimes a man aims high, and all goes well.

A people sometimes will step back from war;
elect an honest man; decide they care
enough, that they can't leave some stranger poor.
Some men become what they were born for.

Sometimes our best efforts do not go
amiss; sometimes we do as we meant to.
The sun will sometimes melt a field of sorrow
that seemed hard frozen: may it happen for you.

SHEENAGH PUGH (b. 1950)

The Passionate Shepherd to his Love

Come live with me, and be my love,
And we will all the pleasures prove
That valleys, groves, hills and fields,
Woods, or steepy mountain yields.

And we will sit upon the rocks,
Seeing the shepherds feed their flocks
By shallow rivers, to whose falls
Melodious birds sing madrigals.

And I will make thee beds of roses,
And a thousand fragrant posies,
A cap of flowers, and a kirtle,
Embroidered all with leaves of myrtle.

A gown made of the finest wool
Which from our pretty lambs we pull,
Fair lined slippers for the cold,
With buckles of the purest gold.

A belt of straw and ivy buds,
With coral clasps and amber studs,
And if these pleasures may thee move,
Come live with me, and be my love.

The shepherds' swains shall dance and sing
For thy delight each May-morning;
If these delights thy mind may move,
Then live with me, and be my love.

CHRISTOPHER MARLOWE (1564–93)

Letter to André Billy. 9 April 1915

Gunner/Driver One (front-line)
Here I am and send you greetings
No no you're not seeing things
My Sector's number fifty-nine

I hear the whistle o_f
the $_{ey}$ the bird
beautiful bird of p^r

I see^{far} aw$_{ay}$ O   D
the $_{cathedral}$ H   E
                        M   A
                        Y   A   R
                        N   D   R   E
                        B   I   L   L   Y

GUILLAUME APOLLINAIRE (1880–1918)

translated by OLIVER BERNARD

Child

Your clear eye is the one absolutely beautiful thing.
I want to fill it with colour and ducks,
The zoo of the new

Whose names you meditate –
April snowdrop, Indian pipe,
Little

Stalk without wrinkle,
Pool in which images
Should be grand and classical

Not this troublous
Wringing of hands, this dark
Ceiling without a star.

SYLVIA PLATH (1932–63)

A song for England

An' a so de rain a-fall
An' a so de snow a-rain

An' a so de fog a-fall
An' a so de sun a-fail

An' a so de seasons mix
An' a so de bag-o'-tricks

But a so me understan'
De misery o' de Englishman.

ANDREW SALKEY (b. 1928)

Letters from Yorkshire

In February, digging his garden, planting potatoes,
he saw the first lapwings return and came
indoors to write to me, his knuckles singing

as they reddened in the warmth.
It's not romance, simply how things are.
You out there, in the cold, seeing the seasons

turning, me with my heartful of headlines
feeding words onto a blank screen.
Is your life more real because you dig and sow?

You wouldn't say so, breaking ice on a waterbutt,
clearing a path through snow. Still, it's you
who sends me word of that other world

pouring air and light into an envelope. So that
at night, watching the same news in different houses,
our souls tap out messages across the icy miles.

MAURA DOOLEY (b. 1957)

The Bonnie Broukit Bairn

Mars is braw in crammasy,
Venus in a green silk goun,
The auld mune shak's her gowden feathers,
Their starry talk's a wheen o' blethers,
Nane for thee a thochtie sparin',
Earth, thou bonnie broukit bairn!
– *But greet, an' in your tears ye'll drown*
The haill clanjamfrie!

HUGH MACDIARMID (CHRISTOPHER MURRAY GRIEVE)
(1892–1978)

braw: fine

crammasy: crimson

a wheen o' blethers: a pack of nonsense

broukit: neglected

greet: weep

the haill clanjamfrie: the whole caboodle

'Music, when soft voices die'   Shelley's draft, extensively revised.
Bodleian Library MS Shelley adds. e.8, p.154 rev. By permission of The
Bodleian Library, University of Oxford.

To Emilia V –

Music, when soft voices die,
Vibrates in the memory –
Odours, when sweet violets sicken,
Live within the sense they quicken.

Rose leaves, when the rose is dead,
Are heaped for the beloved's bed –
And so thy thoughts, when thou art gone,
Love itself shall slumber on . . .

PERCY BYSSHE SHELLEY (1792–1822)

Concerto for Double Bass

He is a drunk leaning companionably
Around a lamp post or doing up
With intermittent concentration
Another drunk's coat.

He is a polite but devoted Valentino,
Cheek to cheek, forgetting the next step.
He is feeling the pulse of the fat lady
Or cutting her in half.

But close your eyes and it is sunset
At the edge of the world. It is the language
Of dolphins, the growth of tree-roots,
The heart-beat slowing down.

JOHN FULLER (b. 1937)

THERE I SAT VIEWING THE SILVER STREAMS
GLIDE SILENTLY TOWARDS THEIR CENTRE THE
TEMPESTUOUS SEA. IZAAK WALTON 1593-1683.

THE RIVER COLNE
UXBRIDGE

21 *The River Colne, Uxbridge* **Alfred France** 1911

When daffodils begin to peer
With heigh! the doxy over the dale
Why, then comes in the sweet o' the year

Shakespeare

THE DAFFODILS ARE OUT—
WHAT ABOUT YOU?

22 *The Daffodils are Out* **Dorothy Hutton** 1939

Spring goeth all in white,
Crowned with milk-white may:
In fleecy flocks of light
O'er heaven the white clouds stray:

White butterflies in the air;
White daisies prank the ground:
The cherry and hoary pear
Scatter their snow around.

ROBERT BRIDGES

23 *'Spring goeth all in white'* **Gregory Brown** 1940

UNDERGROUND

GOLDERS HILL PARK.

*Now fades the glimmering landscape on the sight
And all the air a solemn stillness holds.*
Gray.

Book to
GOLDER'S GREEN.

24 *Book to Golder's Green* **T. R. Way** 1911

Words, Wide Night

Somewhere on the other side of this wide night
and the distance between us, I am thinking of you.
The room is turning slowly away from the moon.

This is pleasurable. Or shall I cross that out and say
it is sad? In one of the tenses I singing
an impossible song of desire that you cannot hear.

La lala la. See? I close my eyes and imagine
the dark hills I would have to cross
to reach you. For I am in love with you and this

is what it is like or what it is like in words.

CAROL ANN DUFFY (b. 1955)

The Lobster Quadrille

'Will you walk a little faster?' said a whiting to a snail,
'There's a porpoise close behind us, and he's treading on my tail.
See how eagerly the lobsters and the turtles all advance!
They are waiting on the shingle – will you come and join the dance?
   Will you, won't you, will you, won't you, will you join the dance?
   Will you, won't you, will you, won't you, won't you join the dance?

'You can really have no notion how delightful it will be
When they take us up and throw us, with the lobsters, out to sea!'
But the snail replied 'Too far, too far!', and gave a look askance –
Said he thanked the whiting kindly, but he would not join the dance.
   Would not, could not, would not, could not, would not join the dance.
   Would not, could not, would not, could not, could not join the dance.

'What matters it how far we go?' his scaly friend replied.
'There is another shore, you know, upon the other side.
The further off from England the nearer is to France –
Then turn not pale, beloved snail, but come and join the dance.
   Will you, won't you, will you, won't you, will you join the dance?
   Will you, won't you, will you, won't you, won't you join the dance?'

LEWIS CARROLL (1832–98)

The Lobster Quadrille   Illustration by John Tenniel.

'I shall say what inordinate love is'

I shall say what inordinate love is:
The furiosity and wodness of mind,
An instinguible burning, faulting bliss,
A great hunger, insatiate to find,
A dulcet ill, an evil sweetness blind,
A right wonderful sugared sweet error,
Without labour rest, contrary to kind,
Or without quiet, to have huge labour.

ANON. (15th century)

wodness: frenzy

Inordinate love   The only known source of this English version of a well-
known Latin original. Thott 110, 4to., f. 163a. By permission of The
Copenhagen Royal Library.

144

A red red Rose

O my Luve 's like a red, red rose,
  That's newly sprung in June;
O my Luve 's like the melodie
  That's sweetly play'd in tune.

As fair art thou, my bonnie lass,
  So deep in luve am I;
And I will love thee still, my Dear,
  Till a' the seas gang dry.

Till a' the seas gang dry, my Dear,
  And the rocks melt wi' the sun:
I will love thee still, my Dear,
  While the sands o' life shall run.

And fare thee weel, my only Luve!
  And fare thee weel, a while!
And I will come again, my Luve,
  Tho' it were ten thousand mile!

ROBERT BURNS (1759–96)

The Very Leaves of the Acacia-Tree are London

The very leaves of the acacia-tree are London;
London tap-water fills out the fuschia buds in the back garden,
Blackbirds pull London worms out of the sour soil,
The woodlice, centipedes, eat London, the wasps even.
London air through stomata of myriad leaves
And million lungs of London breathes.
Chlorophyll and haemoglobin do what life can
To purify, to return this great explosion
To sanity of leaf and wing.
Gradual and gentle the growth of London Pride,
And sparrows are free of all the time in the world:
Less than a window-pane between.

KATHLEEN RAINE (b. 1908)

One Art

The art of losing isn't hard to master;
so many things seem filled with the intent
to be lost that their loss is no disaster.

Lose something every day. Accept the fluster
of lost door keys, the hour badly spent.
The art of losing isn't hard to master.

Then practice losing farther, losing faster:
places, and names, and where it was you meant
to travel. None of these will bring disaster.

I lost my mother's watch. And look! my last, or
next-to-last, of three loved houses went.
The art of losing isn't hard to master.

I lost two cities, lovely ones. And, vaster,
some realms I owned, two rivers, a continent.
I miss them, but it wasn't a disaster.

– Even losing you (the joking voice, a gesture
I love) I shan't have lied. It's evident
the art of losing's not too hard to master
though it may look like (*Write* it!) like disaster.

ELIZABETH BISHOP (1911–79)

To Someone Who Insisted I Look Up Someone

I rang them up while touring Timbuctoo,
Those bosom chums to whom you're known as *'Who?'*

X. J. KENNEDY (b. 1929)

NOTES TO THE POEMS

Up in the Morning Early   'The chorus of this song is old; the two stanzas are mine' (Burns's note).

33   **The Trees**   Philip Larkin was on the Compton Poetry Fund committee when it approved a grant which enabled us to pay for the first year of advertising spaces on the Underground. He took a special interest in the project and wrote to us with useful suggestions: 'I have always liked the Wayside Pulpit placards (''Don't Put Your Wishbone Where Your Back-bone Ought To Be''), and think it might be equally inspiring to be able to read on a tube journey poems that served as a reminder that the world of the imagination existed . . . What level of appreciation are you aiming at? Somerset Maugham, in his play-writing days, said that if you saw the audiences' taste in terms of the alphabet, it was best to aim at letter O. I don't think it would hurt to remind people of poems they already know; not everyone will know them.' Shortly before his death, he wrote to us again: 'I am glad your project is being favourably regarded; it makes me wonder whether I shall ever actually see one of the poems in the proposed location.' Sadly, he died before the first set of poems was posted.

35   **The Sick Rose**   William Blake, known in his own day as an engraver rather than a poet, published his *Songs of Innocence* and *Songs of Experience* in hand-engraved, hand-coloured editions of his own design ('illuminated printing'). This meant, in effect, that the poems remained virtually unknown until Blake was rediscovered as a great visionary poet in the 1860s. Both 'The Sick Rose' and 'The Tyger' were published in *Songs of Experience* (1794).

37   **At Lord's**   Cricket's laureate is Francis Thompson, whose 'At Lord's' evokes the image of an exiled Lancastrian watching a match at Lord's cricket ground but seeing in his mind's eye a game played elsewhere, many years before. The poem is a reduced version of a longer poem which mentions, as well as the Lancashire batsmen Hornby and

Barlow, Gloucestershire's 'resistless' Grace brothers. When the poster appeared on the Tube, the former cricketer Mike Selvey reprinted it in full in his *Guardian* Cricket Diary ('No, this isn't the arts page – just a bit of our cultural heritage for a change') and we were inundated with requests for the poem, mostly from Lancashire.

41 **Composed Upon Westminster Bridge** 'Written on the roof of a coach, on my way to France' (Wordsworth's note). With Wordsworth's dating of the poem in mind, we arranged a 'workshop' on Westminster Bridge at dawn on 3 September 1986. We advertised in the London listings magazines and to our amazement between twenty and thirty people turned up, including a visiting American professor and the poet Wendy Cope. At dawn (twelve minutes past six, BST) we read the poem aloud. Then we settled down to watch the sun rise and write some poems of our own. Aware that the Thames crosses England from west to east, we gazed downstream, waiting to see the sun. We might have waited a very long time, as on this stretch the Thames runs due north (towards Islington, York and the Arctic circle). In any case, it was an overcast morning. When the sun suddenly gleamed through, apparently to our south, we were mightily surprised. Once we were cold enough, we adjourned to a local coffee shop to warm up and read our poems.

When T. S. Eliot's 'Prelude' was displayed on the Tube, we held a second 'winter' workshop at dusk on Waterloo Bridge, somewhat impeded by rain and sleet.

43 **The Loch Ness Monster's Song** The author explained in conversation that the lonely monster rises from the loch and looks round for the companions of his youth – prehistoric reptiles – and, finding nobody he knows, he descends again to the depths after a brief swearing session. This was confirmed by a nine-year-old boy in a workshop, who said the monster was 'looking for a diplodocus'. When asked how he knew that, he said, 'It says so.' It does.

Some years ago, Edwin Morgan was commissioned by the Scottish Arts Council to write a series of poems for the inauguration of Glasgow's refurbished Underground system. He sent us this sample, which sent such alarm through the Strathclyde transport executive that they decided against using the poems.

The Subway Piranhas

Did anyone tell you
that in each subway train
there is one special seat
with a small hole in it
and underneath the seat
is a tank of piranha-fish
which have not been fed
for quite some time.
The fish become agitated
by the shoogling of the train
and jump up through the seat.
The resulting skeletons
of unlucky passengers
turn an honest penny
for the transport executive,
hanging far and wide
in medical schools.

44   **Living**   On learning that a poem of hers was to appear on the Underground, Denise Levertov, who was born in London but has lived mainly in the United States, wrote to us: 'I am totally thrilled at the idea of having a poem in the Tube. I spent innumerable hours in the Tube from age 12–23, and a good many before and since, too. I am in fact a sort of Tube Rat, like a "rat" of the Paris Opera – a *denizen*. Appearance in American trains and buses means little to me – but London, ah, London! – that's different.'

49   **I Am Becoming My Mother** The title poem of a volume for which Lorna Goodison was awarded the Commonwealth Poetry Prize (Americas region) for 1986.

50   **'Tagus farewell'**   Written in June 1539 in Spain, where Wyatt was Ambassador at the court of Charles V. Wyatt had just been recalled to London by Henry VIII, and the last lines of the poem may reflect some uneasiness at the fate awaiting him at home. The Spanish and Portuguese River Tagus is famous for its gold. Brutus, a descendant of Aeneas, dreamed that he was destined to found a kingdom in Albion.

53   **Lines** *from* **Endymion**   The famous opening lines of a long poem, and the first of a number of extracts in our collection.

54   **Goodbye**   Charlie Parker was an American jazz saxophonist, possibly the greatest of them all, who died in 1955, aged thirty-four.

57   **'So we'll go no more a-roving'**   Written in a letter to Thomas Moore in which Byron admits to over-indulging in carnival festivities: 'The mumming closed with a masked ball at the Fenice, where I went, as also to most of the ridottos, etc., etc., and, though I did not dissipate much upon the whole, yet I find ''the sword wearing out the scabbard'', though I have but just turned the corner of twenty-nine.'

71   **The Coming of Grendel**   Another extract. In this passage from the Old English epic, the monster Grendel (the original inhabitant of the land) closes in on the glittering wine-hall of the colonisers, where he means to wreak terrible havoc. The translation tries to be as literal as possible, while keeping the linguistic feeling of the original, with its resounding alliteration.

75   **Sonnet from the Portuguese**   The sonnets have no Portuguese original; they were written in secret the year before the poet's marriage to Robert Browning and tell the story of their unfolding love. In a letter to Leigh Hunt, Robert Browning explained how he persuaded Elizabeth Barrett Browning to publish these intimate poems: 'I never suspected the existence of those ''Sonnets from the Portuguese'' till three years after they were written. They were shown to me in consequence of some word of mine, just as they had been suppressed through some mistaken word; it was I who would not bear that sacrifice, and thought of the subterfuge of a name.' The sequence of forty-three sonnets appears as the final work in *Poems of Elizabeth Barrett Browning* (1850), immediately preceded by 'Catarina to Camoens' – a love poem addressed by his dying mistress to the great sixteenth-century Portuguese poet. The suggestion is that 'Catarina' may have written the Sonnets as well, though this is not said explicitly – and the poems quickly became among the most celebrated love poems in the English language.

77   **Symphony in Yellow**   The sketch of Wilde was formerly attributed to Whistler, rather than to his wife Beatrice. They were friends and neighbours of Wilde's in Tite Street, Chelsea.

9 **'Sumer is icumen in'**   Robert Graves and Laura Riding comment in
their paper 'On Anthologies': 'Every possible polite explanation is
given in popular anthologies for *verteth* to distract attention from the
poetic meaning that the buck, full of Spring grass, *farteth*, i.e. breaks
wind.' Scholarly debate still rages on this question, but on balance we
agree with Graves and Riding, and have emended our earlier version.

0 **Roundel** *from* **The Parliament of Fowls**   Sung by the assembled
birds at the end of the St Valentine's Day festivities, when each bird has
been happily paired off with its mate. 'The note,' the narrator explains,
'imaked was in France' – home of courtly love, which Chaucer's deli-
cious poem gently parodies.

95 *from* **To the City of London**   The fourth stanza of a seven-stanza
'balade' recited during Christmas week, 1501, at a dinner held by the
Lord Mayor in honour of the visiting Scottish Ambassador. Usually
assumed to be the work of the Scottish poet William Dunbar, who was
in London at the time.

96 **On First Looking into Chapman's Homer**   Composed during
October 1816, at dawn, as Keats walked home to Southwark from Cler-
kenwell, where he had been visiting his former schoolteacher Charles
Cowden Clarke. They had stayed up all night reading Homer in the
magnificent translation of George Chapman.

00 **'I have a gentil cock'**   We have retained the old spelling of 'gentil' to
suggest 'gently bred' or 'aristocratic'. Chanticleer, in Chaucer's *Nun's
Priest's Tale*, is another 'gentil cock', described in similar terms:

> His coomb was redder than the fyn coral,
> And batailled as it were a castel wal;
> His byle was blak, and as the jeet it shoon,
> Lyk asure were his legges and his toon,
> His nayles whitter than the lylye flour,
> And lyk the burned gold was his colour.

(lines 39–44)

03 **Mmenson**   *mmenson:* an orchestra of seven elephant tusk horns used

on state occasions to relate history; *Agades*: a town in the western Sudan; *Sokoto*: a town in what is now northern Nigeria. (Notes by the author.)

104   **Light**   Diane Wakoski felt that the extract from 'The Hitchhikers' which originally appeared on the Underground would represent a distortion of the poem if reproduced in a book, and we were happy to substitute this complete short poem.

106   **'You took away all the oceans and all the room'**   In 1934, after he was discovered to be the author of a bitter satire on Stalin, Mandelstam was arrested and exiled for three years, first to a small town in the Urals, then to the provincial town of Voronezh, where this poem was written. He was rearrested in 1938, and died en route to a labour camp.

110   **Old English Riddle**   Suggested answer: *Bookworm*. This reminds us that bookworms have always been a genuine problem to book owners. This charming riddle is No. 47 in *The Exeter Book*, probably transcribed c. 960–70 and later owned by the first Bishop of Exeter. The riddles vary greatly in subject and style. Many are about the animal kingdom, others are about artefacts and yet others are about the forces of nature – and there is a sprinkling of teasing double entendre, of a type still popular, which leads the reader to imagine two parallel solutions, one obscene, the other innocent.

118   **The Cries of London**   Two stanzas of a broadside ballad in the 'Roxburghe Ballads', a unique collection of songs and ballads printed between 1560 and 1700, collected by Robert, Earl of Oxford, and now in the British Library. The 'cries' can be heard to this day in many traditional London markets.

122   **'Ich am of Irlonde'**   Fragment of a medieval carol, written with other rhymes and doggerel in French and English on a single vellum leaf, now in the Bodleian Library, Oxford. W. B. Yeats uses the lines as a refrain for 'I am of Ireland', in *Words for Music Perhaps*:

> *'I am of Ireland,*
> *And the Holy Land of Ireland,*
> *And time runs on,' cried she.*
> *'Come out of charity,*
> *Come dance with me in Ireland.'*

26 **The Uncertainty of the Poet** 'The Tate Gallery yesterday announced that it had paid £1 million for a Giorgio de Chirico masterpiece, The Uncertainty of the Poet. It depicts a torso and a bunch of bananas' – *Guardian*, 2 April 1985. *With a Poet's Eye: A Tate Gallery Anthology*, for which the poem was first commissioned, presents paintings and poems side by side.

27 **'I saw a Peacock with a fiery tail'** In his anthology *Come Hither* (1923), Walter de la Mare comments: 'So may the omission of a few commas effect a wonder in the imagination.' The first printing we were able to find was in *Westminster Drollery, Or, A Choice Collection of the Newest Songs and Poems both at Court and Theaters*, by A Person of Quality (1671). There the verse is headed: 'These following are to be understood two ways', and commas half-way through each line encourage the reader to pick up the double meaning. We have followed later editors in omitting the commas.

30 **On Himself** The poet has been profoundly deaf since the age of seven, following an attack of scarlet fever. This poem appeared on the Underground in September 1991. A 1992 collection of David Wright's poems includes these moving lines:

An Appearance of Success

> Some verses, written when he was alive,
> A poster broadcast on the Underground;
> My life (an actor plays him) televised;
> Fame of a kind, if not recognition;
> Pleasing enough but not enough to please
> An unambitiousness at seventy-one,
> Or pierce the unawareness of the dead:
> This present I'd have loved to give to him
> To make amends,
> – My father – an appearance of success
> In his deaf difficult son;
> Something to recompense
> As may have seemed to him
> Rewardless and too long a sacrifice.

132   **The Passionate Shepherd to his Love**   Because of limited space, in our Underground poster we adapted the four-stanza version published in *The Passionate Pilgrim* (1599). The six-stanza version published in *England's Helicon* (1600) has been reprinted ever since in this form, often with its companion piece, 'The Nymph's Reply to the Shepherd' by Sir Walter Raleigh:

> If all the world and love were young,
> And truth in every shepherd's tongue,
> These pretty pleasures might me move
> To live with thee and be thy love.
>
> Time drives the flocks from field to fold,
> When rivers rage and rocks grow cold,
> And Philomel becometh dumb;
> The rest complains of cares to come.
>
> The flowers do fade, and wanton fields
> To wayward winter reckoning yields;
> A honey tongue, a heart of gall,
> Is fancy's spring, but sorrow's fall.
>
> Thy gowns, thy shoes, thy beds of roses,
> Thy cap, thy kirtle, and thy posies
> Soon break, soon wither, soon forgotten, –
> In folly ripe, in reason rotten.
>
> Thy belt of straw and ivy buds,
> Thy coral clasps, and amber studs,
> All these in me no means can move
> To come to thee and be thy love.
>
> But could youth last and love still breed,
> Had joys no date nor age no need,
> Then these delights my mind might move
> To live with thee and be thy love.

133   **Letter to André Billy**   During the First World War, Apollinaire served in the French artillery and infantry. He survived a skull wound towards the end of the war, but died a few months later in the influenza

epidemic ravaging Paris. In a letter to his friend André Billy, he wrote of his *Calligrammes*: 'They are an idealization of *vers-libre* poetry and of typographical precision at a time when typography is brilliantly ending its career, at the dawn of new methods of reproduction, the cinema and the gramophone.' In the original French text, typography is used to suggest the shape of a bird of prey (as a shell), an eye, and a cathedral (specifically, Notre Dame).

Poème epistolaire

Premier canonnier conducteur
Je suis au front et te salue
Non non tu n'as pas la berlue
Cinquante-neuf est mon secteur

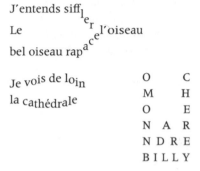

39   **To Emilia V –**   Mary Shelley discovered these lines after Shelley's death in one of his notebooks, when she was transcribing his poems for publication. The manuscript draft which we reproduce, the only known source of the poem, was composed at the same time as the opening lines of *Epipsychidion*, Shelley's celebration of love. The same images appear in both texts: music, memory, rose leaves (or petals).

> Sweet Spirit! Sister of that orphan one,
> Whose empire is the name thou weepest on,
> In my heart's temple I suspend to thee
> These votive wreaths of withered memory.

Poor captive bird! who, from thy narrow cage,
Pourest such music, that it might assuage
The rugged hearts of those who prisoned thee,
Were they not deaf to all sweet melody;
This song shall be thy rose: its petals pale
Are dead, indeed, my adored Nightingale!
But soft and fragrant is the faded blossom,
And it has no thorn left to wound thy bosom.

(1–12)

Teresa Emilia Viviani, to whom these lines were addressed, was the daughter of the Governor of Pisa. Shelley, who lived in Pisa in 1821–22, visited her in the convent where she was awaiting an arranged marriage, and he took a deep interest in her fate. She wrote sonnets and an essay on Love, a sentence of which Shelley uses as an epigraph to *Epipsychidion* ('Verses addressed to the noble and unfortunate lady, Emilia V –, now imprisoned in the convent of –'). 'Music, when soft voices die' also pays a compliment to Emilia's writings, the 'thoughts' which, when their author is gone, Love itself shall slumber on. Shelley's editors, following Mary Shelley, entitle the lines 'To –', which we have expanded on the suggestion of the manuscript evidence.

142   **The Lobster Quadrille**   From *Alice in Wonderland*. This poem, which parodies Mary Howitt's ' "Will you walk into my Parlour?" said the spider to the fly', is sung to Alice by the Mock Turtle, while he and his friend the Gryphon 'solemnly' dance on the sea-shore, a moment magically captured by Sir John Gielgud and Malcolm Muggeridge in Jonathan Miller's television version of *Alice*.

144   **I shall say what inordinate love is**   'Inordinate' rather than lawful love is the subject of this lyric. In the original MS, the poem is accompanied by a briefer Latin original (which also appears elsewhere). The Latin treats merely of *Amor* (love), rather than the inordinate variety:

Dicam quid sit Amor: Amor est insania mentis
Ardor inextinctus, insaciata fames
Dulce malum, mala dulcedo, dulcissimus error
Absque labore quies, absque quiete labor.

Of the many English variations on this theme during the Renaissance, probably the most famous is Shakespeare's defintion of 'lust' in Sonnet 129:

> Mad in pursuit, and in possession so;
> Had, having, and in quest to have, extreme;
> A bliss in proof, and proved, a very woe,
> Before, a joy proposed; behind, a dream.

145 **A red red Rose** Burns copied out a slightly different version of this song in a letter to his friend Alexander Cunningham, describing it as 'a simple old Scots song' which he had picked up in the country. Virtually every stanza of the song can be matched in oral tradition and earlier broadside ballads, and Burns's editors disagree on the extent to which he may have altered or improved it. But the final version seems unmistakably to have his special touch, in its tenderness and lyricism and its impeccable rhythms.

NOTES TO THE POSTERS

following page 28

1 **Pied Piper** ('For he led us, he said, to a joyous land') From 'The
Pied Piper of Hamelin' by Robert Browning, Stanza 13. Spoken 'in after
years' by the lame boy who was left behind – the only child to survive.

2 **The Only Way to the Theatres** ('Jest and youthful jollity') From
'L'Allegro' by Milton, lines 26–32. The poem celebrates the joys of the
cheerful and sociable life, which are contrasted with the melancholy
pleasures of solitude in a companion poem, 'Il Penseroso'. The quoted
passage, addressed to the goddess Mirth, begins:

> Haste thee nymph, and bring with thee
> Jest and youthful jollity . . .

and continues:

> Come, and trip it as ye go
> On the light fantastic toe,
> And in thy right hand lead with thee
> The mountain nymph, sweet Liberty.
>
> (11. 25–6, 33–6)

3 **'As we dance round a-ring-a-ring'** Anon., from Walter de la
Mare's delightful anthology *Come Hither* (1923), No. 16. De la Mare
attributes this 'traditional rhyme' to his old friend 'Mr Nahum' and his
scrapbook; like other pieces found in the scrapbook, it may be by de la
Mare, at least in part. The full text follows:

> As we dance round a-ring-a-ring,
> A maiden goes a-maying;
> And here a flower, and there a flower,
> Through mead and meadow straying:

O gentle one, why dost thou weep? –
Silver to spend with; gold to keep;
Till spin the green round World asleep,
And Heaven its dews be staying.

4   **'Over the land freckled with snow half-thawed'** 'Thaw', by
Edward Thomas. A four-line poem, quoted in its entirety, missing only
its title.

following page 60
Humours of London A series which uses poetic tags in ways best
described as 'tongue-in-cheek'.

5   **At the Shops** ('Getting and spending, we lay waste our powers')
The line quoted comes from a sonnet by Wordsworth, written in
1802–4, one of his most impassioned attacks on the materialism of his
age.

> The world is too much with us; late and soon,
> Getting and spending, we lay waste our powers:
> Little we see in Nature that is ours;
> We have given our hearts away, a sordid boon!
> This Sea that bares her bosom to the moon;
> The winds that will be howling at all hours,
> And are up-gathered now like sleeping flowers;
> For this, for every thing, we are out of tune;
> It moves us not. – Great God! I'd rather be
> A Pagan suckled in a creed outworn;
> So might I, standing on this pleasant lea,
> Have glimpses that would make me less forlorn;
> Have sight of Proteus rising from the sea;
> Or hear old Triton blow his wreathèd horn.

6   **'Appy 'Ampstead** This fragment is from *Oh! 'Ampstead!*, a music-
hall song written well before the turn of the century. John Crook wrote
the music; the words are by Albert Chevalier, the popular cockney
comedian, famous for his coster routines and songs, including
'Knocked·'em in the Old Kent Road' and 'My Old Dutch'. Arthur
Symons, the '90s poet, dubbed Chevalier 'the Costers' Laureate'. The
entire song, of which we print the first verse and chorus, presents a
lively portrait of Hampstead Heath fair in late Victorian times.

Now if yer want a 'igh old time,
　　Just take a tip from me.
Why 'Ampstead, 'appy 'Ampstead,
　　Is the place to 'ave a spree.
You parker wiv dinarlies
　　An' I'm willin' for to bet
The day you spent at 'Ampstead 'Eath
　　You never will forget.

Chorus:　Oh, 'Ampstead! 'Appy, 'appy 'Ampstead;
　　　All the doners look so nice;
　　　Talk about a Paradise.
　　Oh, 'Ampstead's very 'ard to beat.
　　If you want a beano it's a fair old treat!

'Doners' (or 'donnas') are girls or young women; 'dinarlies' is money (from 'denarius', the 'd' of £.s.d.); 'parker wiv' is 'part with' (in context, 'place a wager').

7　**At the Proms**　('Unfit for treasons, stratagems, and spoils')
Adapted from Shakespeare, *The Merchant of Venice*, V.1, 83–8.
　　The man that hath no music in himself,
　　Nor is not mov'd with concord of sweet sounds,
　　Is fit for treasons, stratagems, and spoils;
　　The motions of his spirit are dull as night,
　　And his affections dark as Erebus:
　　Let no such man be trusted. Mark the music.

8　**Up River**　('Where the silent river glides')　To illustrate the chaos of rowboats jostling for space 'up river', the ingenious Underground copy-writer adapted lines from 'The Voice of Nature' by Robert Bridges (in *Shorter Poems*, Book III):

　　But far away, I think, in the Thames valley,
　　　The silent river glides by flowery banks . . .

following page 76
Flowers and Forests　The poetic extracts used in this series, like the idyllic scenes portrayed so sensuously by the poster artist, E. McKnight Kauffer, describe nature in its most lush and inviting aspect. We offer here a sample of the darker side.

9   **Flowers of the Riverside**   ('And nearer to the river's trembling edge')   From 'The Question' by Shelley, Stanza 4. The flowers are imagined or dreamed, rather than seen. Stanza 5 supplies the characteristic melancholy twist:

> Methought that of these visionary flowers
>   I made a nosegay, bound in such a way
> That the same hues, which in their natural bowers
>   Were mingled or opposed, the like array
> Kept these imprisoned children of the Hours
>   Within my hand, – and then, elate and gay,
> I hastened to the spot whence I had come,
> That I might there present it! – Oh! to whom?

10   **Flowers o' the Corn**   ('Flowers fresh in hue')   From *Childe Harold's Pilgrimage* by Byron, Canto IV, Stanza 117. The lines describe the dwelling of the fountain nymph, Egeria, wise counsellor to the Roman king Numa:

> Flowers fresh in hue, and many in their class,
>   Implore the pausing step, and with their dyes
> Dance in the soft breeze in a fairy mass;
>   The sweetness of the violet's deep blue eyes,
> Kiss'd by the breath of heaven, seems coloured by its skies.

Byron contrasts this innocent erotic scene with the realities of human passion:

> Alas! our young affections run to waste,
>   Or water but the desart; whence arise
> But weeds of dark luxuriance, tares of haste,
>   Rank at the core, though tempting to the eyes,
> Flowers whose wild odours breathe but agonies,
>   And trees whose gums are poison; such the plants
> Which spring beneath her steps as Passion flies
>   O'er the world's wilderness, and vainly pants
> For some celestial fruit forbidden to our wants.

(Stanza 120)

11   **Blue Bells, Kew Gardens**   ('Dark bluebells drenched with dews of summer eves')   From *The Scholar Gypsy* by Matthew Arnold, line 88.

Arnold's poem is based on the story of a seventeenth-century student who left Oxford and joined a band of gypsies. The poet imagines the 'scholar gypsy' still haunting the countryside near Oxford, and contrasts the image of a vanished past with the anxieties of Victorian England:

> O born in days when wits were fresh and clear,
>   And life ran gaily as the sparkling Thames;
>   Before this strange disease of modern life,
>   With its sick hurry, its divided aims,
>   Its heads o'ertaxed, its palsied hearts, was rife –
>   Fly hence, our contact fear!

(lines 201–6)

12 **The Forest Glades of Epping** ('Overhead the tree tops meet') From *Pippa Passes*, by Browning, Act IV. The opening lines of a song sung by Pippa, a girl from the silk mills, on her New Year's holiday, in which she imagines herself in turn as one of the 'Happiest Four' in the town of Asolo:

>   For am I not, this day,
>   Whate'er I please? What shall I please to-day,
>   My morn, noon, eve and night – how spend my day?
>   To-morrow I must be Pippa who winds silk,
>   The whole year round, to earn just bread and milk:
>   But, this one day, I have leave to go,
>   And play out my fancy's fullest games . . .

Pippa's song is overheard by the Monsignor and his attendants, just as they are plotting to abduct her and install her as a courtesan in Rome, having discovered that she is the illegitimate child of Monsignor's eldest brother. Her song softens the heart of Monsignor, who immediately repents – and Pippa, unaware of the beneficent influence her singing has had on all who overhear it, returns to her labours in the silk mill. Her last thoughts before falling asleep summarize the democratic philosophy that appealed so much to the Victorians:

> All service ranks the same with God –
> With God, whose puppets, best and worst,
> Are we: there is no last nor first.

following page 92
Home Counties A series with a strong conservationist flavour, urging Londoners to explore the countryside north, south, east and west of the city.

13   **Essex** ('The Wayside is open to all')   The opening words of 'Nightingale Road', an essay in *Nature near London* (1883), by Richard Jefferies. Jefferies, one of the great observers of rural life in England, was born in Wiltshire in 1848 and died of tuberculosis at the age of 38. He had an almost mystical feeling for nature, heightened by his illness and described in his strange autobiographical work, *The Story of My Heart*.

14   **Bucks** ('What is this life, if full of care')   The first two couplets of 'Leisure', an oft-anthologized poem by William H. Davies (1871–1940).

15   **Surrey** ('Here are the chalk and the sand')   From *Rural Rides* (1830) by the agitator and propagandist William Cobbett, one of the first investigative journalists and an ardent lover of rural England. Between 1821 and 1832 he traversed the counties of England on horseback, recording his observations in his journal. This description of Surrey is taken from an entry of 23rd October, 1825:

'Thursley, four miles from Godalming, Surrey . . . I who have seen so many, many towns, think [Guildford] the prettiest, and, taken all together, the most agreeable and most happy-looking that I ever saw in my life. Here are hill and dell in endless variety. Here are the chalk and the sand, vieing with each other in making beautiful scenes. Here is a navigable river and fine meadows. Here are woods and downs. Here is something of everything but *fat marshes* and their skeleton-making agues.'

His stated purpose was 'to see the people without any disguise or affectation' and 'to gain real knowledge as to their situation' – which was often grim, in this period of acute agricultural distress. *Rural Rides* thus contrasts the beauty of the English countryside with the hardship caused by increased urbanization, the displacement of farming people from their small independent holdings, and the Government's refusal to repeal the onerous Corn Laws. Whether Cobbett would have welcomed being quoted in a London Underground poster is open to doubt. He says in a journal entry for 27th March 1826: '[I] am convinced that the *facilities* which now exist for *moving human bodies from place to place* are amongst the *curses* of the country.' (His italics.)

16 **Kent** ('Hops, Reformation, Bays, and Beer') Quoted in *A Tour through England and Wales* (1724–26), by Daniel Defoe, Letter 2. Referring to the Maidstone district of Kent, Defoe writes:

'Here likewise, and in the country adjacent, are great quantities of hops planted, and this is called Mother of Hop Grounds in England; being the first place in England where hops were planted in any quantity . . . These were the hops, I suppose, which were planted at the beginning of the Reformation, and which gave occasion to that old distych:

Hops, Reformation, bays, and beer,
Came into England all in a year.'

The OED cites a prose version from 1654: 'They were wont to say here, that Peacocks, Hops, and Heresie, came first into England in one and the same ship.' Izaak Walton quotes yet another version in *The Compleat Angler*, taken from Sir Richard Baker's *Chronicle of the Kings of England* (1653), who writes in his account of the reign of Henry the Eighth: 'About his 15th year, it happened that divers things were newly brought into England, whereupon this Rhyme was made:

Turkeys, Carps, Hoppes, Piccarel,and Beer,
Came into England all in one year.'

(We present these variant forms for those curious to see how a rhyme may go a progress from a chronicle of kings through a travel guide into the bowels of the London Underground.)

following page 124
The Proud City This 1944 series presents London sites which suffered severe bomb damage during the blitz of 1940–41. The artist, Walter Spradbery, said they were intended to convey 'the sense that havoc itself is passing and with new days come new hopes.' German

bombing raids had resumed in January 1944, and in June the first raids of the 'secret weapon', the V1s, the 'flying bombs' or 'doodlebugs', began. At the same time, Allied forces under Bomber Command were continuing the saturation bombing of German cities.

17   **St. Paul's** ('The principal Ornament of our royal City')   From the preamble to the royal warrant authorizing Sir Christopher Wren's designs for the rebuilding of St Paul's Cathedral, which had been virtually destroyed in the Great Fire of 1666. During the 1941 blitz the great dome of St Paul's, Wren's masterpiece, had been left intact, despite the heavy damage suffered in the immediate vicinity, as Spradbery's poster eloquently testifies.

18   **St. Clement Danes**   ('Where the fair columns of St. Clement stand') From *Trivia: Or, The Art of Walking the Streets of London* (1716) by John Gay. The lines quoted are from Book III, 'Of walking the Streets by Night', lines 17–18. There follow accounts 'Of Pick-Pockets', 'Of Ballad-Singers', 'Of crossing the Street', 'Of Oysters', 'Of avoiding Paint', 'Of various Cheats formerly in practice', 'How to Recognize a Whore', and, amongst other categories, 'The Happiness of London'. St. Clement Danes was gutted by fire in 1941, and was restored after the war as the headquarters church of the Royal Air Force.

19   **Temple Church and Library**   ('So may the Winged Horse . . still flourish')   From 'The Old Benchers of the Inner Temple' by Charles Lamb, in *Essays of Elia* (1823). In this essay Lamb laments the disappearance from the Inner Temple Hall of the marble relief of the Winged Horse, by the eminent Dutch sculptor John Michael Rysbrack. This 'badge and cognizance' of the Inner Temple had formerly been visible from Crown Office Row, where Lamb was born and lived for his first seven years. Rysbrack's Winged Horse, removed in 1810, was rediscovered and set up in the new Library in 1871, where it was treated to several coats of paint. In the 1930s the marble relief, restored to its former glory, was installed over the entrance to the Hall. The Hall was destroyed in the 1941 bombing raids, but the Winged Horse survived. When the Temple buildings were repaired after the war, the Winged Horse was placed over the entrance to the Benchers' rooms on Church Court, where it can be seen, by appointment, to this day.

20 **Chelsea Power House** ('the poor buildings lose themselves in the dim sky') From James McNeill Whistler's 'Ten O'Clock Lecture', a statement of aesthetic principles given at Prince's Hall in February 1885. Whistler, who lived in Chelsea, saw the city with the eye of an artist, and his 'nocturnal' vision of the riverside, captured in atmospheric paintings and drawings, must have seemed ironically prophetic when the city was suffering nightly bombing raids:

> 'And the evening mist clothes the riverside with poetry, as with a veil, and the poor buildings lose themselves in the dim sky, and the tall chimneys become campanili, and the warehouses are palaces in the night, and the whole city hangs in the heavens, and fairy-land is before us –'

following page 140

21 **The River Colne, Uxbridge** ('There I sat viewing the silver streams') From *The Compleat Angler* (1653) by Izaak Walton, Part 1, Chapter iv. This charming account of the joys of angling (and of the contemplative life) is also a compendium of poetry, including Marlowe's 'Passionate Shepherd' and Raleigh's 'Reply', George Herbert's 'Vertue', and the distich about Hops quoted above, Poster 16.

22 **The Daffodils are Out** ('When Daffodils begin to peer') The opening lines of a song from Shakespeare's *Winter's Tale*, IV.ii.1–12. Sung by Autolycus, a stealer of sheets with a taste for bawdy:

> When daffodils begin to peer,
>   With heigh! the doxy, over the dale,
> Why, then comes in the sweet o' the year;
>   For the red blood reigns in the winter's pale.
>
> The white sheet bleaching on the hedge,
>   With heigh! the sweet birds, O, how they sing!
> Doth set my pugging tooth on edge;
>   For a quart of ale is a dish for a king.
>
> The lark, that tirra-lirra chants,
>   With heigh! with heigh! the thrush and the jay,
> Are summer songs for me and my aunts,
>   While we lie tumbling in the hay.

169

23 **'Spring goeth all in white'** An untitled poem by Robert Bridges, in *Shorter Poems*, Book IV; quoted in full.

24 **Book to Golder's Green** ('Now fades the glimmering landscape on the sight') Two lines from one of the best-known poems in the English language, 'Elegy Written in a Country Churchyard' by Thomas Gray. The churchyard of the title was in Stoke Poges in Buckinghamshire, about thirty miles northwest of Golders Green.

INDEX OF POETS, AUTHORS AND TRANSLATORS

Numbers in **bold** refer to the posters

Adcock, Fleur 19, 48
Angelou, Maya 121
Apollinaire, Guillaume 133, 156–7
Arnold, Matthew **4**, **11**, 164–5
Auden, W. H. 80

Baker, Sir Richard 167
Benson, Gerard 71, 110
Bernard, Oliver 133
Berry, James 34
Bishop, Elizabeth 147
Blake, William 19, 35, 87, 149
Brathwaite, Edward Kamau 103
Bridges, Robert **8**, **23**, 21, 163, 170
Brown, Clarence 106
Browning, Elizabeth Barrett 75, 152
Browning, Robert **1**, **12**, 21, 152, 161, 165
Burns, Robert 18, 25, 145, 149
Byron, George Gordon, Lord **10**, 21, 57, 152, 164

Carroll, Lewis 142
Causley, Charles 108
Chaucer, Geoffrey 90, 153
Chapman, George 153
Chevalier, Albert **6**, 162
Clarke, Gillian 70
Cobbett, William **15**, 166–7
Coleridge, Samuel Taylor 128
Cope, Wendy 19, 126, 150

Davies, William H., **14**, 165
de la Mare, Walter **3**, 47, 155, 161
Defoe, Daniel **16**, 167
Dickinson, Emily 36

Donne, John 19, 45
Dooley, Maura **16**, 136
Drayton, Michael 19, 115
Duffy, Carol Ann 141
Dunbar, William 19, 95, 153

Eliot, T. S. 68, 150
Ewart, Gavin 120

Fainlight, Ruth 76
Feinstein, Elaine 112
Finch, *see* Winchilsea
Forché, Carolyn 65
Fuller, John 140

Gay, John **18**, 168
Goodison, Lorna 49, 151
Graves, Robert 113, 152
Gray, Thomas **24**, 170
Grieve, Christopher Murray
  see MacDiarmid, Hugh

Hardy, Thomas 83
Hass, Robert 93
Heaney, Seamus 28
Herbert, Cicely 89
Herbert, George 111, 169
Herrick, Robert 91
Hopkins, Gerard Manley 63
Housman, A. E. 19, 116
Howitt, Mary 158
Hughes, Ted 114
Hulme, T. E. 124

Jefferies, Richard **13**, 166

Jennings, Elizabeth 88

Kavanagh, Patrick 107
Keats, John 18, 19, 53, 96, 153
Kennedy, X. J. 148
Kipling, Rudyard 97

Lamb, Charles **19**, 168
Larkin, Philip 33, 149
Lawrence, D. H. 102
Lear, Edward 19, 62
Levertov, Denise 44, 151
Lim, Shirley Geok-lin 98
Lochhead, Liz 19, 60
Logue, Christopher 69

MacCaig, Norman 125
MacDiarmid, Hugh 137
McGough, Roger 19, 94
MacNeice, Louis 129
Mahon, Derek 64
Mandelstam, Osip 106, 154
Marlowe, Christopher 132, 169
Maugham, Somerset 149
Merwin, W. S. 106
Millay, Edna St. Vincent 92
Milligan, Spike 19, 58
Milosz, Czeslaw 93
Milton, John **2**, 19, 21, 61,
    161
Mitchell, Adrian 54
Morgan, Edwin 43, 150

Nichols, Grace 19, 29

Plath, Sylvia 134
Pugh, Sheenagh 131

Raine, Kathleen 146
Raleigh, Sir Walter 156, 169
Rich, Adrienne 109
Riding, Laura 152
Roethke, Theodore 117

Salkey, Andrew 135
Sassoon, Siegfried 42
Satyamurti, Carole 82
Shakespeare, William **7**, **22**, 21, 30,
    66, 159, 163, 169
Shelley, Mary 157
Shelley, Percy Bysshe **9**, 18, 21, 26,
    139, 157–8, 164
Smith, Ken 39
Smith, Stevie 19, 32
Soyinka, Wole 59
Stevenson, Anne 55
Symons, Arthur 162

Tennyson, Alfred, Lord 21, 123
Thomas, Dylan 72
Thomas, Edward **4**, 51, 162
Thomas, R. S. 81
Thompson, Francis 37, 149–50
Tsvetayeva, Marina 112

Viviani, Teresa Emilia 158

Wakoski, Diane 104, 154
Walcott, Derek 73
Walton, Izaak **21**, 167, 169
Whistler, James McNeill **20**, 169
Whitman, Walt 101
Wilde, Oscar 77, 152
Williams, William Carlos 19, 27
Winchilsea, Anne Finch, Countess of
    46
Wordsworth, William **5**, 19, 21, 41,
    150, 162
Wright, David 130, 155
Wright, Judith 38
Wright, Kit 99
Wyatt, Sir Thomas 50, 151

Yeats, W. B. 31, 154

Anonymous: **4**, **16**, 40, 56, 79, 84,
    100, 118, 122, 127, 144

INDEX OF FIRST LINES

Numbers in **bold** refer to the posters

	Page
A cool small evening shrunk to a dog bark and the clank of a bucket	114
A moth, I thought, munching a word	110
A thing of beauty is a joy for ever	53
Above all rivers thy river hath renown	95
Abstracted by silence from the age of seven	130
An omnibus across the bridge	77
An' a so de rain a-fall	135
And yet the books will be there on the shelves, separate beings	93
Ann, Ann!	47
As we dance round a-ring-a-ring	**3**, 161
Aunt Jennifer's tigers prance across a screen	109
Broad sun-stoned beaches	73
Cauld blaws the wind frae east to west	25
Come live with me, and be my love	132
Come, wed me, Lady Singleton	32
Death be not proud, though some have called thee	45
Did anyone tell you	151
Earth has not anything to show more fair	41
Earth in beauty dressed	31
English Teeth, English Teeth!	58
Everyone suddenly burst out singing	42
Everything changes. We plant	89
Full fathom five thy father lies	66
Gunner/Driver One (front-line)	133
He breathed in air, he breathed out light	54
He is a drunk leaning companionably	140

Here we are all, by day; by night we're hurled   91
Here's fine rosemary, sage, and thyme   118
Hirsute hell chimney-spouts, black thunderthroes   59
Hops, Reformation, Bays, and Beer   167
How do I love thee? Let me count the ways   75

I am a poet   126
I am of Ireland   122
I could not dig: I dared not rob   97
I have a gentil cock   100
I have eaten   27
I have known the inexorable sadness of pencils   117
I know the truth – give up all other truths!   112
I live for books   104
I met a traveller from an antique land   26
I rang them up while touring Timbuctoo   148
I saw a jolly hunter   108
I saw a Peacock with a fiery tail   127
I shall say what inordinate love is   144
I tell a wanderer's tale, the same   39
I wanna be the leader   94
I want him to have another living summer   120
If all the world and love were young   156
In either hand the hast'ning angel caught   61
In February, digging his garden, planting potatoes   136
In London   29
In my craft or sullen art   72
In Spanish he whispers there is no time left   65
In the gloom of whiteness   51
Into my heart an air that kills   116
It is little I repair to the matches of the Southron folk 37

Last night I dreamt in Chinese   98
Last night in London Airport   69
Love without hope, as when the young bird-catcher   113

Many policemen wear upon their shoulders   99
Margaret, are you grieving   63

Mars is braw in crammasy 137
Much have I travell'd in the realms of gold 96
Much Madness is divinest Sense 36
Music, when soft voices die 139
My beloved spake, and said unto me, Rise up, my love, my fair one,
    and come away 105
My first is in life (not contained within heart) 60
My mother's old leather handbag 76

November '63: eight months in London 48
Now from the marshlands under the mist-mountains 71
Now sleeps the crimson petal, now the white 123
Now welcome Summer with thy sunnè soft 90

O my Luve 's like a red, red rose 145
O Rose thou art sick 35
Once, in finesse of fiddles found I ecstasy 124
Only a man harrowing clods 83
Over the land freckled with snow half-thawed **4**, 162

Rain on lilac leaves. In the dusk 70

Since there's no help, come let us kiss and part 115
So we'll go no more a-roving 57
Softly, in the dusk, a woman is singing to me 102
Some verses, written when he was alive 155
Sometimes things don't go, after all 131
Somewhere on the other side of this wide night 141
Spring goeth all in white **23**, 170
Sssnnnwhuffffll? 43
Stop all the clocks, cut off the telephone 80
Sumer is icumen in 79
Summon now the kings of the forest 103
Sweet day, so cool, so calm, so bright 111
Sweet spirit! Sister of that orphan one 157

Tagus farewell, that westward with thy streams 50
Thanks to the ear 34
The art of losing isn't hard to master 147

The birds sang in the wet trees   107
The fire in leaf and grass   44
The forest drips and glows with green   38
The Frost performs its secret ministry   128
The grey sea and the long black land   67
The highway is full of big cars   121
The radiance of that star that leans on me   88
The room was suddenly rich and the great bay-window was   129
The salmon lying in the depths of Llyn Llifon   81
The silver swan, who living had no note   56
The trees are coming into leaf   33
The very leaves of the acacia-tree are London   146
The winter evening settles down   68
The world is too much with us; late and soon   162
There was an Old Man with a beard   62
They won't let railways alone, those yellow flowers   55
Trail all your pikes, dispirit every drum   46
Trees are cages for them: water holds its breath   125
Two sticks and an apple   84
Two women, seventies, hold hands   82
Tyger Tyger, burning bright   87

Western wind when wilt thou blow   40
What am I after all but a child, pleas'd with the sound of my own
    name? repeating it over and over   101
What lips my lips have kissed, and where, and why   92
When daffodils begin to peer   **22**, 169
When I am sad and weary   54
When in disgrace with Fortune and men's eyes   30
When we climbed the slopes of the cutting   28
'When you stop to consider   64
'Will you walk a little faster?' said a whiting to a snail   142

Yellow/brown woman   49
You took away all the oceans and all the room   106
Your clear eye is the one absolutely beautiful thing   134

A NOTE OF THANKS

'POEMS ON THE UNDERGROUND' could not have prospered without the continued help and cooperation of London Underground. We are also grateful for financial support from the Calouste Gulbenkian Foundation, the Arts Council of Great Britain, Greater London Arts, the Stefan Zweig Programme of The British Library, Queen Mary and Westfield College (University of London), the Esmée Fairbairn Foundation, J. Rothschild Holdings and Sotheby's. Support from publishers has come not only from Faber and Faber Ltd and Oxford University Press but also from Virago, W. W. Norton, Jonathan Cape, Century Hutchinson, Chatto and Windus, and Grafton Books. We have been particularly fortunate in our designers, and are grateful to Pentagram for providing the original design; to students at the London College of Printing, especially Mark Lissak and Jane Graham, for designing a second series; and to Tom Davidson, who has designed our posters from 1989 to 1992.

For their invaluable help in the preparation of the illustrated edition we join the publishers in thanking Paul Castle, of the London Transport Museum, and the staff of the LTM Archives.

The number of friends and colleagues who have generously given encouragement and practical advice is too great to list here – to all, our thanks.

ACKNOWLEDGEMENTS

The editors and publisher gratefully acknowledge permission to reproduce the following copyright poems in this book:

Fleur Adcock: 'Immigrant' from *Selected Poems* (1983), © Fleur Adcock 1983. Reprinted by permission of Oxford University Press.

Maya Angelou: 'Come. And Be My Baby' from *Just Give Me A Cool Drink of Water 'Fore I Diiie*, © Maya Angelou 1971. Reprinted by permission of Virago Press.

W. H. Auden: Song ('Stop all the clocks, cut off the telephone') from *Collected Poems* by W. H. Auden, © W. H. Auden 1968. Reprinted by permission of Faber and Faber.

Gerard Benson: 'The Coming of Grendel' from *Beowulf*, and 'Old English Riddle', © Gerard Benson 1988 and 1990. Reprinted by permission of the author.

Oliver Bernard, translator: 'Letter to André Billy. 9 April 1915' from Guillaume Apollinaire, *Selected Poems* (1986), translation © Oliver Bernard 1986. Reprinted by permission of Anvil Press.

James Berry: 'Benediction' from *Chain of Days* (1985), © James Berry 1985. Reprinted by permission of Oxford University Press.

Elizabeth Bishop: 'One Art' from *Complete Poems 1927–1979*, © Alice Helen Methfessel 1983. Reprinted by permission of Farrar, Straus and Giroux.

Edward Kamau Brathwaite: 'Mmenson' from *The Arrivants* (1973), © Edward Kamau Brathwaite 1973. Reprinted by permission of Oxford University Press.

Charles Causley: 'I Saw a Jolly Hunter' from *Figgie Hobbin* © Charles Causley 1970. Reprinted by permission of Macmillan Publishers and David Higham Associates.

Gillian Clarke: 'Taid's Grave' from *Selected Poems*, © Gillian Clarke 1985. Reprinted by permission of Carcanet Press.

Wendy Cope: 'The Uncertainty of the Poet' from *With a Poet's Eye: A Tate Gallery Anthology* (1986), © Wendy Cope 1986. By permission of Faber and Faber.

Walter de la Mare: 'Alas, Alack!' from *Peacock Pie*. Reprinted by permission of The Literary Trustees of Walter de la Mare and The Society of Authors as their representative.

Emily Dickinson: 'Much Madness is divinest Sense' from *The Poems of Emily Dickinson*, ed. Thomas H. Johnson, © The President and Fellows of Harvard College 1955, 1983. Reprinted by permission of Harvard University Press.

Maura Dooley: 'Letters from Yorkshire' from *Explaining Magnetism* (1991), © Maura Dooley 1991. Reprinted by permission of Bloodaxe Books.

Carol Ann Duffy: 'Words, Wide Night' from *The Other Country*, © Carol Ann Duffy 1990. Reprinted by permission of Anvil Press.

T. S. Eliot: 'Prelude I' from *Collected Poems 1909–1962* by T. S. Eliot, © T. S. Eliot 1963, 1964. Reprinted by permission of Faber and Faber.

Gavin Ewart: 'A 14-Year-Old Convalescent Cat in the Winter' from *The New Ewart: Poems 1980–1982*, © Gavin Ewart 1982. Reprinted by permission of Hutchinson.

Ruth Fainlight: 'Handbag' from *Selected Poems*, © Ruth Fainlight 1987. Reprinted by permission of Century Hutchinson.

Elaine Feinstein, translator: 'I know the truth' from Marina Tsvetayeva, *Selected Poems* (1971), translation © Elaine Feinstein 1971. Reprinted by permission of Olwyn Hughes.

Carolyn Forché: 'The Visitor' from *The Country Between Us* (1981), © Carolyn Forché 1981. Reprinted by permission of Jonathan Cape.

John Fuller: 'Concerto for Double Bass' from *Selected Poems 1954–1982*, © John Fuller 1985. Reprinted by permission of the author.

Lorna Goodison: 'I Am Becoming My Mother' from *I Am Becoming My Mother* (1986), © Lorna Goodison 1986. Reprinted by permission of New Beacon Books.

Robert Graves: 'Love Without Hope' from *Collected Poems* (1975) by Robert Graves. Reprinted by permission of A. P. Watt on behalf of The Trustees of the Robert Graves Copyright Trust.

Seamus Heaney: 'The Railway Children' from *Station Island* by Seamus Heaney, © Seamus Heaney 1984. Reprinted by permission of Faber and Faber.

Cicely Herbert: 'Everything Changes', © Cicely Herbert 1989. Reprinted by permission of the author.

Ted Hughes: 'Full Moon and Little Frieda' from *Wodwo* by Ted Hughes, © Ted Hughes 1982. Reprinted by permission of Faber and Faber.

Elizabeth Jennings: 'Delay' from *Collected Poems* (1967). © Elizabeth Jennings 1986. Reprinted by permission of David Higham Associates.

Patrick Kavanagh: 'Wet Evening in April' from *The Complete Poems of Patrick Kavanagh*, © Peter Kavanagh 1972. Reprinted by permission of Peter Kavanagh.

X. J. Kennedy: 'To Someone Who Insisted I Look Up Someone' from *Cross Ties: Selected Poems* (1985), © X. J. Kennedy 1985. Reprinted by permission of University of Georgia Press.

Philip Larkin: 'The Trees' from *High Windows* by Philip Larkin, © Philip Larkin 1974. Reprinted by permission of Faber and Faber.

Denise Levertov: 'Living' from *Selected Poems* (1986), © Denise Levertov 1986. Reprinted by permission of Bloodaxe Books and New Directions.

Shirley Geok-lin Lim: 'Modern Secrets' from *Modern Secrets*, © Shirley Geok-lin Lim 1989. Reprinted by permission of Dangaroo Press.

Liz Lochhead: 'Riddle-Me-Ree' from *Dreaming Frankenstein and Collected Poems* (1984), © Liz Lochhead 1984. Reprinted by permission of Polygon Books.

Christopher Logue: 'London Airport' from *Ode to the Dodo. Poems 1953–1978* by Christopher Logue, Jonathan Cape/Turret Books, © Christopher Logue 1981. Reprinted by permission of the author.

Norman MacCaig: 'Stars and planets' from *Tree of Strings* (1977), © Norman MacCaig 1977. Reprinted by permission of Chatto & Windus.

Hugh MacDiarmid: 'The Bonnie Broukit Bairn' from *The Complete Poems of Hugh MacDiarmid*, (Penguin 1985). Reprinted by permission of Mr Michael Grieve and Martin Brian & O'Keeffe.